Themes for Educational Gymnastics

SECOND EDITION

JEAN WILLIAMS MA.,Dip.P.E.
Principal Lecturer and Head of Studies
in Human Movement, Trinity and All
Saints Colleges, Horsforth, Leeds

LEPUS BOOKS · LONDON

Copyright © 1979 Henry Kimpton (Publishers) Ltd
7 Leighton Place, Leighton Road, London NW5 2QL

First edition 1974
    Reprinted 1976
Second. edition 1979

ISBN 0 86019 038 2

British Library Cataloguing in Publication Data

Williams, Jean, b. 1924
    Themes for educational gymnastics.—2nd ed.
    1. Gymnastics—Study and teaching
    I. Title
    796. 4'1   GV461

Printed in Great Britain at the
University Press, Cambridge

CONTENTS

Foreword   vii

The system outlined

  1 Introduction   1
  2 The Aims of Educational Gymnastics   6
  3 The Concept of a Theme   16
  4 Analysis of a Theme   25
  5 Example of Analysis of a Theme—Balance and Overbalance   43
  6 Structuring Individual Lesson Plans   53
  7 Use of Apparatus   59

Examples of themes

  1 Locomotion and Pause   Introductory   78
  2 Weight-bearing   "   84
  3 Transference of Weight   "   88
  4 Use of Feet and Legs   "   96
  5 Changes of Speed   "   102
  6 Flight   Intermediate   108
  7 Body Shape   "   116
  8 Partner Work   "   122
  9 Twisting and Turning   "   128
10 Rising and Falling *by Margaret Talbot*   "   135
11 Levels and Directions   "   140
12 Use of Hands and Arms   "   147
13 Swinging *by Margaret Talbot*   Advanced   154
14 Symmetry and Asymmetry *by Margaret Talbot*   "   159
15 Threes and Small Groups   "   165
16 Rhythmic Patterns   "   171

Conclusion   178

References   179

Index   181

ACKNOWLEDGEMENTS

Margaret Talbot, of Trinity and All Saints' Colleges, has contributed three new themes for this edition, and I am grateful for her valuable additions.

I am also indebted to Professor H.T.A. Whiting of the Vrije University, Amsterdam, who encouraged me to expand my lecture notes to form this book. Mrs Irene Glaister (recently Lecturer in Physical Education at Leeds University) gave me constant encouragement and offered her cheerful fortitude in the face of many verbal attacks in the course of the clarification of my ideas. I have been greatly helped by Miss E. Mauldon, recently Vice-Principal of Lady Mabel College of Education, Rotherham, particularly with reference to the theme in Partner Work, and by Miss Jennifer Drake, M.A., presently Adviser to Hampshire Education Authority, who patiently modified my English, my punctuation and my more outlandish ideas. David Kelly designed the key and made beautiful diagrams from doodlings and scraps of paper when he was a student of interior design at the Royal College of Art. Ted Grinham, College Photographer, and students of Trinity and All Saints' Colleges provided material for illustrations. Indeed I am totally indebted to the Human Movement students at Trinity and All Saints' Colleges who, over the years, have produced such exciting work and who have convinced me, by their practise in schools, of the great value of educational gymnastics to boys and girls and all age levels.

Jean Williams

FOREWORD

While there are no clear-cut criteria of when a second edition of a book should be written, it is usually felt by the author that its contribution could be increased if new material were added and if the conceptual framework in which it is placed be brought into line with current thinking. Both criteria have been adopted in this revised text.

Educational gymnastics has suffered in the past from the failure of its exponents to justify their claims in terms of empirical evidence or educational theory. Fortunately such evidence is now becoming available, although there is still a considerable way to go. Nevertheless it is hoped that the production of empirical evidence will lead to the development of theoretical systems which can be tested in the applied field. Such a reciprocal relationship between theory and practice is the only way that useful progress can be made. With this in mind, Jean Williams has written an extensively reviewed chapter on the aims of educational gymnastics for this second edition which attempts to discuss the psychological literature on skill acquisition and performance in as far as it has meaning for the practise of educational gymnastics. That such a literature does not provide a complete framework is all too obvious. The reader will, however, be impressed by the links which can be made and the way in which they provide some justification for the methods outlined in the chapters which follow.

Throughout, the text has been carefully revised but inevitably the large section on themes and their application, which was based on the author's very considerable experience as teacher and practitioner, is little changed. However, three very valuable additional themes have been added to this edition. They are by Margaret Talbot, who is an experienced teacher of educational gymnastics. The new themes are designed to help in developing fluent transitions from one spatial level to another (rising and falling), in the smooth transference of weight from one part of the body to another (swinging), and in the development of accuracy in symmetrical and asymmetrical movements. Margaret Talbot writes :

> Jean Williams' book has provided the 'scaffolding' she intended from which many students and teachers of gymnastics have built their work.
>
> I had been introduced to a thematic approach to gymnastics during my own student days and had developed and refined the structures

then used while teaching schoolchildren; but the rigour and logic underlying this book has helped me to clarify my ideas and has allowed me to develop new themes in response to students' needs. Three of them (rising and falling; swinging; and symmetry and asymmetry) now form part of this second edition. I hope that students and teachers will be encouraged to add to gymnastics material in the same way.

This then is a justification of the success of Jean Williams' original concept. *Themes on Educational Gymnastics* is a book about action. It encourages readers to be involved; to think, to plan, to develop. It gives its readers a handhold by which they may climb to greater heights of achievement. As such, it is a challenge—a challenge to progress.

H.T.A. Whiting

THE SYSTEM OUTLINED

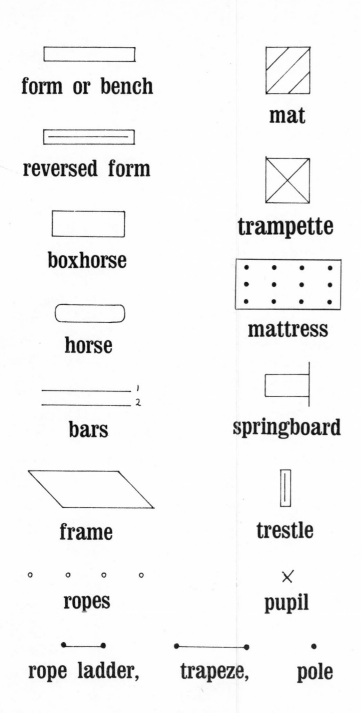

form or bench

reversed form

boxhorse

horse

bars

frame

ropes

rope ladder,   trapeze,   pole

mat

trampette

mattress

springboard

trestle

pupil

It is suggested that students use tracings from the key opposite to design apparatus settings.

1 INTRODUCTION

Educational gymnastics is a term applied to a form of gymnastics taught in schools. It is based on traditional gymnastics, of which Olympic gymnastics is the paradigm example. In content there are similarities, but in practice educational gymnastics is more loosely structured and has a completely different methodology.

Similarities in content include the basic forms of gymnastic movement in balance, fall and flight and in their elaboration in sequences. Anatomical and mechanical analyses in both cases would reveal similarities of body action. Performance in both cases regards logical structure of sequences and their aesthetic properties as crucial. Differences are emphasised by the context in which the two forms are practised, in their aims and objectives and in their method of teaching.

Olympic gymnastics is essentially competitive and is judged by set criteria. The aim is to win and objectives are concerned with sequences of action which include set skills which are specific to the sport. These are rated according to difficulty and to the accuracy with which they are performed. The method of teaching is one of training individual skills, and the sequences made by combining these skills are frequently determined by the coach. The individual thus conforms to externally imposed movement patterns which he practises to as near a perfect performance as possible.

Where educational gymnastics is taught it normally forms an integral part of the physical education programme in schools. Children are taught in their school classes which are determined by age and not by sex, size, skill or physical aptitude. The aim is to develop skill but always in the context of the ability and understanding of the individual pupil. Knowledge about the activity and its practical application in problem-solving situations are considered as important as standards of performance. Experience and conceptualisation are parallel aims. The method of teaching is generally one of guided discovery and self-selection within the limits and freedoms of a general objective. Educational gymnastics is a form of movement in which everyone can find meaning and satisfaction and some understanding of their own movement ability.

1

For the teacher of physical education, gymnastics is only one area of study. He must also be an expert in swimming, diving, life-saving, all major games, athletics, dance and, nowadays, show competence in water and mountaineering sports as well. Small wonder that in six hours a week for three years—which is the average time for main course work—some areas become neglected. Teachers need source material to which they can refer quickly, which is structured clearly and which will help them in the rush and ever-changing situations which arise in physical education departments of large schools. Such material is not easily available at present in the areas of gymnastics and dance.

It has been thought for many years that detailed lesson plans given to students would tend to make their work stereotyped and superficial. Experience shows that this depends on the individual student and that some students are likely to become stereotyped anyway. It is better that they should have a variety of material to which they may refer, than that they should have to rely on that which they can recall, often years later, from college experience. Other students will use this material as it is intended: as a series of ideas for starting-points in the development of their own material for teaching. Lack of such backing-up material causes some young teachers to give up teaching educational gymnastics after the first term and many, who meet this work in college for the first time, go back to their own formal school experience when faced with a practical teaching situation.

The purpose of this book is to provide a scaffolding which the teacher can use to structure his own schemes of work. The material will be analysed into themes. A theme will be broken down into the basic elements which may be applied to the development of an idea and which point to the definition of units of work. Lesson plans, based on the units of work, will be suggested. The outline of a series of lessons forming a module of work using a theme as a basis will be given. Thus it is hoped to provide a model for the application of a movement idea and its development into a series of lessons in the gymnasium.

The book also contains examples of the model. These examples are based on the work of one teacher and her students and it is not claimed that all the possible material of educational gymnastics is included. The idea of this book is not to be encyclopaedic but to stimulate ideas and discussion and, perhaps, to encourage those who would not otherwise try to begin work in the exciting and varied field of educational gymnastics. The examples provide guidelines, but only guidelines, for the use of the teacher. From these it is hoped he will branch out and develop his own work in his own situation and from his own experience.

His own experience is vital as a source of information. One cannot learn about movement only by reading books. One cannot learn to teach by

THEME

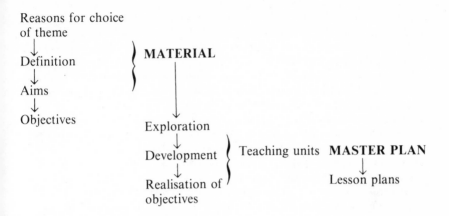

Reasons for choice
of theme
↓
Definition
↓
Aims
↓
Objectives

MATERIAL
↓

Exploration
↓
Development
↓
Realisation of
objectives

Teaching units   MASTER PLAN
↓
Lesson plans

Fig. 1. The basic model for a theme.

going to lectures. Teaching is a complex activity involving the teacher learning and analysing what he learns, the teacher observing and analysing what he sees and the teacher structuring experiences for children as a result of these analyses. The teacher also learns by his own continuing work; he learns about gymnastics by working himself. He should do all he can to enlarge his experience of the doing, the taking part, so that his own sense of the feel of bodily movement stays alert to the problems and pleasures of accepting physical challenges. This experience, together with a growing knowledge of the material, will help him to judge wisely when he comes to select tasks for his classes.

The teacher also learns by observation. He is constantly observing and assessing a changing situation in the gymnasium. He is at the same time watching the whole class and individuals. As a result of his awareness of the mood, problems or successes of the class as a whole, he decides on the timing and definition of the next task or comment. At the same time he is noting and mentally recording the reactions of some individuals and, where possible, giving individual help. Within the class there will be a wide variety of mental and physical ability and the teacher learns by watching the different ways individuals cope with the same task. He helps and encourages them to overcome their particular weaknesses and exploit their strengths. As the teacher and class grow in mutual confidence, the teacher shares the results of his observation with the class, teaching them how to see, so directing their attention that they too learn by watching each other.

The use of film and video-tape can be useful here. To watch others moving, whether they be Olympic champions or peers engaged in the same learning process, adds to the store of knowledge and experience of the body in movement. This store is extended in several ways by such observation. First, the variety of movement ideas is increased. In the exploration of new tasks not only bodily experience is needed but also both suggestions from the teacher and visual stimulation. Secondly, film affords the opportunity to see beautiful and highly skilled movement and, therefore, it helps children to identify form and clarity. Film may lead to discussion of points of technique, of action of body parts, of timing in thrust and resilience, and rhythm and flow of movement. Observation is of major importance in increasing vocabulary of movement both for teacher and pupils and film and video-tape provide valuable source material.

So this book is only a skeleton which some students may use as a foundation for the teaching process. An attempt is made to reduce the material of gymnastic movement to its elements. The purpose is not to discuss methods of teaching, although these may impinge on the use of material in certain situations, but to put before the student a range of possible starting points on which to base his teaching. Furthermore, the aim is to clarify a procedure by which the student can build his own schemes of work. In short, the objectives of the book are:-

1. To discuss the aims of educational gymnastics.
2. To clarify the concept of a theme.
3. To analyse a theme.
4. To illustrate this analysis with examples
5. To structure lesson plans, with examples.

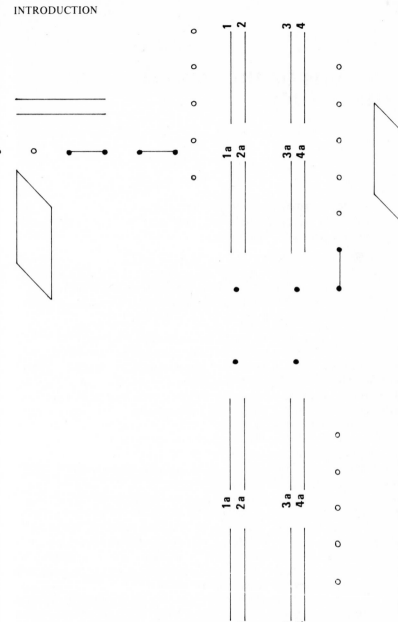

Fig. 2. Plan of gym (fixed apparatus in position).

2 THE AIMS OF EDUCATIONAL GYMNASTICS

Educational gymnastics is an activity in which the attention of the performer is focused immediately and completely on the movement of his own body. As Ricoeur (1966) says

> Here I am concerned exclusively with my body; I make movements which are movements for nothing, in order to exercise my body. They correspond to a highly artificial and purely preparatory study in which results do not count, and in which the moral, professional and social context of the work disappears.

In other words in gymnastics the movement is undertaken for its own intrinsic value. The body becomes the object of attention and action. In other forms of physical education physical skill is directed towards extrinsic objectives. In games it is directed towards the strategy of team play in order to win; in dance, attention is focused on communicative or aesthetic objectives and in athletics on competing against oneself or others. In gymnastics bodily skill is developed as an end in itself. The attention of the gymnast is on the flexibility, strength and beauty of his own movement. The action itself is the aim and content of the work whereas in other forms of physical education the action is incidental (though necessary) to other aims.

It is claimed that the practise of educational gymnastics makes a significant contribution to the development of a person's body awareness and body concept. These terms refer to the individual's appreciation and knowledge of his own body. Educational gymnastics also develops movement awareness and movement concepts. This claim implies that the student both knows how and is able to select and perform the appropriate movement responses to situations which demand action. Movement concepts are built up through the process of skill learning, which results in the formulation of movement schemata relating to a variety of movement types. Movement concepts are extended and tested by working through a variety of problem-solving situations in which it is necessary to assess the task and provide an adequate solution. The response having been determined, the student is then required to reach a high level of performance such that an aesthetic appreciation of excellence, even in the simplest solutions, is developed.

The aims of educational gymnastics may be summarised as follows:-

1. To develop body awareness and body concept.
2. To develop skill through the learning of skills.
3. To develop movement concepts through the utilization of skills in problem-solving situations.
4. To foster an aesthetic appreciation of excellence in body movement.

1. Body awareness and body concept

Underlying the notions of body awareness and body concept is the idea of the physiology of the *body schema*. This term was first used by Head (1920) when he described the schema as a structure of networks of nerve fibres which relay sensory information to the brain relating to body position and movement. The brain stores the information in the form of a dynamic diagram of the body, 'a storehouse of past impressions'. This is used as a standard against which incoming information is judged. Head emphasises the unconscious nature of the schema when he says

> ...for this combined standard, against which all subsequent changes of posture are measured before they enter consciousness, we propose the word schema...

The schema is in continuous physiological process, undergoing persistent modification of structure as new information enters the system. The schema must be continuously flexible, keeping a tally on the state of the body. Head uses the terms 'spatial schemata' and 'postural schemata' referring to the separate physiological structures which support separate psychological functions.

Bartlett (1932) accepted Head's theories and elaborated the functions of body schemata. His ideas are similar to those of Piaget (Piaget & Inhelder 1958) in his analysis of the formation of structures of knowledge. Both men describe organisations of sensory information which are in an active state, monitoring and regulating mechanisms of body and thought. They are reinforced and strengthened by constant activity, modified by new experience. They also act as a directing factor in the recognition, classification and assimilation of new information. The development of a variety of schemata through learning is an unconscious process. The deliberate structuring of learning programmes by teachers will therefore help to control the formation of new schemata by the students.

(i) Body awareness

Body awareness denotes a sense of appropriateness, sensitivity and competence in bodily movement. Many people are naturally endowed with the potential to develop these qualities and they move economically and easily without fully appreciating their skill. Others only acquire good movement habits through careful training and practice. In either case, work in educational gymnastics affords opportunities to develop body awareness further.

It has been said (Nash 1970) that the most accurate sources of bodily awareness are from haptic and kinaesthetic cues. Educational gymnastics requires the contact of all surfaces and parts of the body with the floor, apparatus and other bodies. It demands the body experience of contraction, extension and twisting of the whole or of parts in the negotiation of apparatus situations. Apparatus provides small and large surfaces for balance, soft surfaces for falling and rolling, small and large gaps, stable and unstable bars and poles, angles, swings and loops. A gamut of haptic experiences are thus provided for the whole body in a variety of ways.

Kinaesthetic information refers to sensations derived internally from the muscles and joints and it supplements visual and tactile sensory inputs. The method of teaching educational gymnastics with its constant emphasis of 'feeling' the movement, sensing the position of parts of the body, 'meeting the floor' with fine touch before transferring weight and so on, is deliberately aimed at increasing body awareness and sensitivity. The teacher questions the class thus: 'What shape are you making?' 'What part of the body leads the movement?' 'Can you feel the line of the body right to the ends of your toes?' Such questions are intended to reinforce and remind students of the 'feel' of movement and to alert them to the sensory apparatus of their body.

(ii) Body concept

Body awareness can only be acquired through a wide range of movement experience and is a mode of knowing as yet not fully articulated by consciousness. Body concept is precisely this articulation. Body concept is tested by what a person can say or draw about his own or other peoples' bodies (Bennett 1960). It is the conscious correlate of body schema and body awareness.

> To form a concept it is necessary to abstract, to single out elements apart from their totality in the concrete experience in which they are embedded (Vygotsky 1962).

The body concept, distilled from a person's total body experience is a blend of the experience of *BEING* a body and *KNOWLEDGE* of the history, shape, size and skills of that same body. The concept is never fully mature.

As Meredith (1966) pointed out a concept is not a static phenomenon:-

> The concepts themselves are ameoboid creatures, extruding their way
> to other concepts, engulfing them absorbing them, resting awhile busy
> with internal growth, occasionally splitting up into daughter concepts,
> full of inheritance and liable to mutation, each a unique individual at
> certain times, but losing itself in others when its separation fails.

The body concept can therefore be continually affected by the experiences of movement. Attention to the kind and quality of the movement experienced is likely to affect body concept, and ultimately will control the formation of good or bad movement behaviour.

2. Skill and skills

(i) Skill

First it is necessary to distinguish between performance and skill. Performance is the manifestation of skill, which is an abstract concept. In other words skill is a psychological construct inferred from performance. Morgan (1974) suggests that skill is a power over action. Ricoeur as early as 1966 noted that every decision implies the skill and ability to carry it out. A decision to take the car shopping implies the skill to drive the car. Skill is implicit in the decision to act. Ryle (1949) goes further:-

> A person' performance is said to be skilful, if in his operation he is
> ready to detect and correct lapses, to repeat and improve successes, to
> profit from examples of others...he performs critically.

This implies intelligent action, thinking while doing. Skill is not a steering by a prior intellectual operation, or a present plan, but a process of thought in action. Performance which can be recorded and measured is the external evidence of skill. Skill is immanent in action. It involves the intention to act, the assessment of immediate body environment circumstances, the recollection of similar instances in the past, the determination of the correct responses, the selection of the motor programme which carries out the response and the monitoring system which adjusts the response in relation to the success or failure of the action taken. In this series of events the carrying out of the action, the effector mechanism, is crucial to the success of the intention. It is at this point that specific skills come into play, the effector mechanism is the learned specific skill by which the intention is completed – thus an accumulation of specific motor skills serves the more general disposition of skill – the distinction is made here between skill as a disposition, and specific motor skills which are body actions in their executive capacity.

(ii) Specific skills

A skill is a learned response, in the form of a motor programme, which is in effect an automated movement habit. A movement habit, such as driving or eating, once had to be learned slowly and painfully in circumstances demanding full attention and effort. The programme runs itself without the need for conscious control, but here it must be noted that the habit never becomes like a reflex action. It can always be commandeered and made subservient to conscious control at any moment. The best example is probably that of postural habits: of sitting, standing and walking. In normal life constant changes of position occur while thinking of other things; for example in conversation it is possible to walk about, sit down, get up without disturbing the train of thought. Concentration on postural activity is not necessary, though it is possible, at any moment. It is a habit which once took much time to learn. What is more, this skill, or habit, adjusts itself to changing circumstances without the need for conscious control. No two movements in everyday living are ever performed in exactly the same circumstances and this flexibility and adjusting process of habit is what Huxley (1938) meant when he referred to the 'body thinking' and what Ricoeur (1966) means when he refers to 'bodily spontaneity'.

So a series of discrete learned skills serve skill, in its organising capacity in human activity.

3. Movement schemata and movement concepts

(i) Movement schemata

Schmidt (1975) has suggested that skill learning may be indexed by a theory of movement schemata. He sees a schema of a movement type (e.g. a forehand drive) as being a stored abstraction of all past experiences of the movement. This schema would operate in the same way as the body schema (see p. 7), in that it would act in recognition and decision processes in determining correct movement responses. According to Schmidt when the individual makes an intentional movement he stores four things:

1. information relating to the body environment situation
2. the specification for the required action
3. the desired outcome, or result of action (imagined)
4. the sensory feedback from the movement (what it feels like)

It is the relationship of these four factors which compose the movement schema. Repeated instances of the movement, or very similar movements will strengthen the schema, which remains in readiness for future use.

Bartlett (1932) discusses the notion of the schema as a means for generating 'novel' responses.

> How I make the (tennis) stroke depends upon the relating of certain

new experiences, most of them visual, to other immediately preceding experiences and to my posture, or to balance of postures, at the moment.

Then, after one takes in this information about the present state of.the body and environment, Bartlett says:

When I make the stroke I do not, as a matter of fact, produce something absolutely new, and I never merely repeat something old.

A movement schema then would be the abstraction from many experiences of similar movements and would be stored in the form of a generalised motor programme. This programme could be adapted and used according to the conditions and specifications determined by the central mechanisms in the brain, in face of a given task. As Bartlett has indicated, no two instances of any movement will ever be exactly the same nor will they ever be entirely different. Tyldesley (1975) refers to 'motor plasticity' indicating the possibility of the adaptable schema, which can be adjusted even during the course of its operation. In the same way that Meredith (1966) speaks of the interaction of mental concepts, it is possible to think of the interaction of movement schemata with each other, and with the postural schemata which remain in overall control of the body in action.

Educational gymnastics, then, is concerned with the organisation of movement experiences. From these experiences, relating to different movement types, the information necessary to initiate, develop and strengthen a variety of movement schemata is derived.

(ii) Movement concepts in gymnastics

One of the stated aims of educational gymnastics is that of developing movement schemata. Movement schemata may be formed through experiences of the basic gymnastic skills of flight, balance, twisting and turning actions, supporting weight on different body parts, body shape, use of feet and legs, rhythmic and tension factors and so on. The work is designed over a period to build up a schema relating to ONE type of movement, which for teaching purposes is referred to as the THEME. The schema is developed by experiencing many instances of the theme on the floor, on apparatus and with partners. The learning is reinforced by the observation of others engaged in the same task, either in class situations or on film or VTR.

A concept has been defined earlier (p. 8) as one instance of the conscious articulation of the state of a schema at a given time. Movement concepts fulfil the same function. One instance of a movement, in a given task, reveals the state of the developing schema which relates to that movement.

The movement conceptualisation is tested by setting tasks related to the experiences. The tasks take the form of movement sequences which the students create and which must answer certain requirements. From the movement they produce it is possible to assess the present state of development of the schema related to the theme. For example in developing a theme on taking the weight over the hands the work follows this pattern:-

1. A variety of movement experiences of taking weight on hands are directed by the tutor. From these a broad movement schema is developed.
2. Analysis of the movement into its component parts of preparation balance and recovery is emphasised. Many different combinations of different recovery and preparation possibilities are experienced under the guidance of the tutor.
3. The awareness and conceptualisation of the schema is brought into consciousness by the construction of individual tasks in the form of sequences. The structure of sequences relating to the theme (in this case the various ways of taking weight over the hands) is articulated by the movement and by critical analysis of the performance.

(iii) The application of movement concepts in problem-solving situations

The setting of task-based objectives in the form of sequences is not only used to test the state of the movement concept. It is also to provide the context in which the individual student may relate the movement concept to his own ability. He discovers what the movement concept means in terms of his own particular body structure and the possibilities and limitations of which control its use. To practise the skill, to understand the elements of the structure of the skill, is not the same thing as coming to terms with his own power to apply it. So alongside the learning of a given schema emphasis is placed on the individual work involving its application. Tasks demanding the employment of the schema in spatial and dynamic situations are set. They are developed by the use of partners, small and large apparatus. The schema is thus learned by the dual method of experience and analysis of the movement in the context of the body and ability of a particular person.

The whole process is clarified by the structuring of objectives.

In realising the objectives the student is required to:-

1. Assess the task in movement terms, e.g.
   How high, how far?
   Which actions?
   How much effort?
2. Select the movement appropriate both to the task and to his own bodily competence.

3. Perform the movement sequence with maximum economy of effort.
4. Practise until a high level of skill is reached in the performance of the sequence.

In the choice of objectives the teacher might be guided by Ryle (1949) who said:-

> Training is not the art of setting tasks which the pupils have not yet accomplished but are not any longer quite incapable of accomplishing.

Examples of the sort of tasks which could be set are given in the objectives section of each theme.

The assumption underlying educational gymnastics is that the development of skill is not an additive process, built up from the perfection of a series of specific actions, but that it consists of a continual reorganisation, reconstruction and renewal of movement schemata akin to Head's body schema relating to the control of posture. It rests on the theory that skilled performance is an intelligent activity in which thought and understanding are immanent. Only when specific actions are so well practised that they are almost machine-like does performance border on the automatic. The balance between skilled behaviour and automatic performance of skills is delicate and dynamic. The learning and practice of too many automatic routines renders movement behaviour stereotyped and rigid. Too little attention to performance and practice leaves movement schemata in a precarious state, weak and unrefined and unable to meet the challenges of new situations. The problem is to find the optimum position in teaching programmes.

The rest of the book is devoted to explanations and examples of teaching skills in context. Students must adapt, adjust, explore and develop each new skill to many different uses as they work through themes. This work demands flexibility of mind and attitude as well as flexibility of body. It is hoped that this combination of thinking while doing will help each student not only to solve successfully the physical problems presented to him in the gymnasium, but also to be alert to the environment in which he lives, and to cope with the physical problems of his daily life.

4. Aesthetic awareness and aesthetic appreciation

In discussion of aesthetics in relation to gymnastics there is no suggestion that an art form is involved. The concern is with the motive form and with the manner of performance. The aesthetic has a dual meaning for the performer as creator, as performer and as critic of his own work, and for the observer as appreciating and appraising it. The factor relevant to both these functions is the determination of criteria by which the movement can be said to have aesthetic value. In formulating criteria the process of structuring form and the subsequent performance will be considered.

(i) Structuring form in gymnastics

In educational gymnastics children are expected to be both composers and performers of their own work. As Wright (1975) has noted in other forms of creative endeavour, children have access to examples of great works from which to learn. Poems, dances, paintings and music all have a literature of their own. In gymnastics, children have only infrequent television programmes which provide examples of excellence. The teacher can help the children here by clarifying frames of reference. The rest of this book contains examples of tasks related to themes, defining both limitations and possibilities inherent in them. The constraints and freedoms of the tasks need careful elaboration. This implies sticking to the point, but also exploring and developing it. Composition involves a process of exploration, selection, modification, rejection, and children need guidelines to help the decision-making implicit in this.

Appropriateness is a key concept here. Are the chosen movements appropriate to the task, to each other in sequence, to the particular body (structure, skill ability), to the apparatus? Is the sequence too long to remember, to sustain, to practise adequately? Does it have a logical flow of movement or does there seem to be unnecessary changes of direction, timing, addition of unnecessary gestures, postures, etc.? Although all these conditions can be fulfilled by anyone, given a suitable movement task, it is obvious that the answers to the questions will be severely limited by the level of skill of the students. Composition is only possible allied to a systematic development of bodily skill through the learning of movement schemata.

The learning of generalised schemata rather than a series of specific gymnastic movements such as a handstand, or flicflac (performed to exact specifications) allows a more flexible understanding of movement. Emphasis is on a logical flow in movement rather than a combination of stunts linked by balletic gestures.

(ii) Performance

Having considered the appropriateness of the form, attention may be given to its design, shape and pattern, both dynamically and spatially. It should be a pleasure to watch, providing aesthetic experience for performer and spectator alike. What factors are important here? Clues may be found in Beardsley's (1970) three criteria of aesthetic 'goodness'; unity, complexity and intensity. Unity and complexity are related in structure. Unity is concerned with the overriding theme, and the elimination of irrelevant movement and gesture. It is also concerned with the overall pattern within the structure, the build-up of material, the beginning and ending or resolution of the sequence. But too much unity becomes tedious, and the variations within the theme and the manner with which they are inserted, interrelated and interwoven is crucial. Intensity is seen more in manner of performance, in emphasis, accelerations, sustainments and in general élan of interpretation. The performance should be exciting, demanding a response from the spectator and satisfaction for the performer. Again, the manner of performance is dependent on the skill of the performer which is only achieved by hard work and constant practise of the refined finished form.

It would be too much to expect that the whole population could be transformed in its everyday movement habits by a course in educational gymnastics, but the hope is that a knowledge and experience of 'good' movement in one context might lead to a desire for it and an appreciation of it in another.

3 THE CONCEPT OF A THEME

The situation in the gymnasium

The movement of the body is so continuous, so inescapable, so inseparable from the experience of living that it is only brought into conscious awareness under certain conditions. These conditions usually arise when the body causes some inconvenience such as failure to negotiate an obstacle, unexpected loss of balance, or when there is pain. Sometimes the body breaks, or is strained when put to an unfamiliar task, but, by and large, man is so accustomed to his physical being that he notices it only when it displeases him. On the occasions when man deliberately tries to achieve any physical skill it is necessary for the mind to direct its attention to the movement of the body. It must record what is happening, analyse this, assess what must be done and give instructions to the body to take action. Yet it is as difficult for man to analyse his own bodily movement as it is to analyse language. He has to use the instrument to study it. In skill learning he is identifying factors in the movement as he is moving. He tries to concentrate on one element in the movement as he is coping with all the other incoming information from stimuli. He must focus attention on one aspect within a total flow of body movement.

For example, many perceptions and impressions are making their impact on a child working in a typical lesson in the gymnasium. He is concerned about the other bodies moving and leaping around him, through which he must thread his own pathway. This need to find his own way in a moving environment is made more of a problem by having to negotiate apparatus as well. It seems to him that his main impressions come through his eyes and his ears but also through his body surfaces, which must be constantly manoeuvred to avoid bumps and knocks. He will be looking up and down and around him, as he makes movement responses to the tasks. As he is working he is listening to a continuous commentary from the teacher, sometimes suggesting ways of answering the task, sometimes commenting on the work of other children or exhorting individuals to more effort for better work. Just as he begins to make some sense out of the

16

situation he is called upon to redirect his attention and co-operate with others in the problem of handling and setting up unwieldy apparatus which at first sight may look frighteningly uninviting. As the lesson proceeds the efforts the child needs to make become more mentally challenging and physically demanding.

This assessment of the child's experience is drawn from the notes of students' observation of individual children taking part in lessons. Many children at first find the gymnasium a bewildering, but exciting experience, but soon settle down to their own interpretation of the situation. In this connection it is interesting to note that while some children act in immediate response to the teacher's voice – others always wait to see what the rest of the class does before they make a move.

While assimilating these visual, auditory and tactile impressions of movement and change, the pupil is expected to learn something about his own movement. He is asked to become kinaesthetically aware. This small internal knowledge from his joints, together with information from the tendons and other sense organs must be brought to his conscious attention. He learns to 'feel' the movement as it is happening. To help the beginnings of this sensory awareness, the first stage in a conscious attempt to develop *body awareness,* some teachers concentrate on one aspect of movement analysis which we shall call the theme.

The situation of the teacher of educational gymnastics is difficult and complex. He knows his aim is to develop 'movement concepts'. He perhaps sees before him, enthusiastic, energetic, ungainly children. His task is not to select certain specific skills which the children can only perform in the limited confines of the gymnasium. Nor is his task solely to strengthen the muscles and mobilise the joints of the body in rotation. If this were so the structuring of schemes of work would be a simple matter of selecting certain exercises according to the particular end in view. Educational gymnastics does not require the pupil to measure his skill against the skill of others, nor does it ask children to endeavour to match up to predetermined feats which may be outside the range of their ability. The task of the teacher is to recognise the present level of skill of each child in his class. Working at first from this, gradually, within general movement patterns selected by each child in the class, the teacher brings into the focal awareness of the individual his own abilities and potential in a wide range of movement experiences. More than that, his task is to develop in the pupil a desire to work hard to raise his level of attainment, to extend the range of his movement and develop his sense of body position and action. Altogether the teacher is faced with a situation of many facets. He does not work from the particular to the general—that is, he does not build up a repertoire of highly specific skills and then adapt and relate them to varying situations. He works from the general to the particular. He takes general movement situations and focuses on the clarification and refinement of chosen aspects of them. It is with the selection of these aspects, themes, and the means of working round them that this book is concerned.

Themes

The theme, then, is a particular aspect of movement chosen by the teacher as the focal point round which he can build a series of lessons. Through a variety of movement experiences given to the class he will gradually emphasise this one element, showing how it is present in many different situations and how it can itself be clarified and developed.

OBJECTIVES OF THEMES

Tasks and sequences

The objectives of the theme are the final pieces of work set by the teacher in connection with the theme. These usually take the form of sequences of movement based on a clear framework set by the teacher. The individual members of the class are free to structure their particular sequences as long as they conform to the framework. Each child will have several finished, practised sequences of movement based on the theme.

To realise the objectives, the teacher will set more specific tasks. The word task refers to the form in which the teacher challenges the class during the lesson. It involves the setting of a unit of work which demands a response from the children. The nature of this response determines the form of the next task. As it is a piece of work given to the whole class, it must allow for the total ability range of the whole group. It should not be too simple or remain unqualified for too long; it must be demanding enough to test the ablest child and yet be answerable by the weakest. Considerable attention should be given to the wording of tasks so that they contain a clear structure of action but never, or rarely, limit the class to a specific movement. Thus in educational gymnastics the command "Cartwheels—begin" would never be given, but the class might be asked to "take your weight on your hands and try to make a wide body shape". A cartwheel would be one possible answer to this task.

Whatever the task, it will be related to a more general objective set by the teacher in connection with the theme. The theme will indicate bodily tasks which will permit a wide range of activity with a focus on only one aspect. For example, the theme could be concerned with twisting and turning, and although many aspects of gymnastics such as travelling, balance, flight and partner work will be used, the emphasis of the teaching will always be on twisting and turning. First, the teacher will clarify the difference between these two actions and then give experiences in how and when these actions occur in the many general activities in the gymnasium. Finally, tasks will be set on large apparatus which will force the body into twisting and turning situations.

The teacher will adjust his work within the theme according to the present needs of the class. The pupil acquires bodily versatility and competence as he works his way through open-ended tasks within which he must indentify and select his own movements and set his own targets. These tasks are carefully structured. They move from exploratory situations, through those demanding selective activities, to a series of set sequences on the floor and on apparatus. The objectives of the theme are realised if the sequences are completed and satisfy the tasks set.

Most gymnastic movements form a 'phrase' in movement. They have a preparation, a climax and a recovery. Thus a jump has a run-up, a take-off, a position in flight and a landing. A sequence of movement occurs when several phrases are linked together to make a 'sentence'. This sentence could have one or more climaxes or just one major emphasis. The sequence may consist of the same movement repeated several times, or of different movements linked together, the recovery of one movement becoming the preparation of the next, so that a continuous flow of movement is achieved. The making of sequences demands considerable skill in the selection and juxtaposition of different movement ideas and a concentration on ways of joining together different parts of the sequence.

The process of selection of material for sequences involves personal choice and is guided and helped by the teacher and by the observation of others engaged in the same process. This operation makes intellectual and aesthetic demands on the child as well as bodily activity. The intellectual component requires the pupil to become conscious of bodily actions, to study and analyse the movements of others, to make decisions and selections and to train movement memory. The aesthetic element involves critical analyses of the form of movement sequences and the refinement and control of their own creative work. Sequences must be learned, practised and brought as near perfection as possible and attention now slides from the particular content of the work to the standard of performance of the individual units of work. The pupil thus gradually builds up a repertoire of gymnastic skills of his own, and if he shows exceptional merit may, if he wishes, proceed to a training squad engaged in more specific forms of work.

CLASSIFICATION OF THEMES

Themes are classified here according to their direction of·focus. They may focus on the GROSS BODY ACTION as it moves across, over, under, through, round, along the floor, partners and apparatus. In answer to tasks the children will have to travel, leap, turn, twist, contract and extend their bodies and so on. These body actions may be performed in a variety of ways (see p.31) and in many different situations. It is through exploration of these ideas that the child begins to 'know bodily'—in Huxley's (1938) sense, the size, shape, flexibility, manoeuvrability of his own body. He learns to judge size, distance, height, angles, shapes in relation to his own capacity to negotiate these. With different parts of the body he learns to grip long narrow shapes, rounded narrow structures, at all angles both unstable and stable, and a variety of textures and surfaces.

As the child becomes competent and fluent in gross body action his attention is drawn to what his body is doing within that action. So a theme connected with PARTS OF THE BODY may be taken. Such a theme brings into focal awareness the function and action of separate body parts. Within the body action the children will be asked to concentrate on one part of the body. For example, the theme may be concerned with the *feet*, how they carry the body across the floor in different ways, thrust it into the air, meet the floor as the body returns; how *feet* behave when the body is supported on other parts, how they can suspend the body from a bar, or support it by gripping a rope. Although the child is using a variety of actions he is thinking about his *feet*, and to him the lesson is about 'feet'.

The third class of themes is concerned with the DYNAMICS of movement. Within the work of the themes connected with action and body parts are other factors which affect the performance of the movement. These deal with the more subtle aspects of control of speed, tension, accent and flow of movement. The same action can be made very quickly or very slowly. In a 'phrase of movement' the accent may come at the beginning, in the middle or at the end. Degrees of body tension may also be experienced in a held position in the air or in balance, for example. Tension difference in take-off and recovery must be experienced so that each pupil will learn to use the optimum amount of energy for the varying tasks in relation to his own body weight and shape.

In this classification are included themes concerned with AWARENESS OF SPACE. These include the experience of handling the body in various spatial contexts. For example, one might land at speed from a height into a small space and immediately change direction to meet a new challenge. Then in contrast to this, one could experience landing from a long leap immediately changing direction. Similarly, the difference in arriving from a trampette high up on a rope is very different from arriving high up in a confined situation—between two bars for example, where the body must contract instead of extending. Apparatus settings which require great flexibility of pathway and of the body would provide contrast to the last two ideas which involve extension and contraction of the body.

Gymnastics is about apparatus: fixed, portable and human. It is about apparatus which is stable and unstable, supportive and ejective, geared to both dangerous and safe situations. Children are brought into bodily RELATIONSHIPS with other people and with a variety of equipment, and in a carefully guided context learn to manage themselves and others. Although these situations are usually structured as developments of other *themes* they can also be used as starting points. For example, a *theme* on lifting, carrying and placing in threes could be taken, the idea being worked out in situations on the floor and with apparatus. In answer to each task the pupil would be required to work in a different group of three pupils and adapt to the variations of size and weight of the other two.

The following list of themes is not intended to be encyclopaedic. It is a list which the author has found useful during some years of teaching. Teachers will want to work out their own list and accentuate the aspects of movement that are important in the context of their own teaching situations.

I. Themes concerned with GROSS BODY ACTION. These include:-

Travelling and stopping
Weight-bearing
Transferring weight from one body part to another
Flight
Body-shape
Twisting and turning
Rising and falling
Swinging
Balance and over-balance

II. Themes concerned with particular BODY PARTS, including:-

Use of hands and arms
Use of legs and feet
Emphasis on body surfaces in rolling, falling and recovery
Relationship of hands and feet to each other
Symmetry and asymmetry

III SPATIAL and DYNAMIC themes such as:-

Levels and directions
Changes of speed
Tension and release

Rhythmic patterns
Spatial patterns in movement and apparatus

IV.   RELATIONSHIPS:-

Partner work   Assisted flight and recovery
Work in threes   Assisted balance
Group work   Taking part or whole weight
                      Lifting, carrying and placing

Themes have been arranged here according to their focus. They have not been graded according to difficulty or complexity. The selection of the right theme is never a simple matter. It is wise to begin work with a new class by taking one or more lessons of a general nature in order to make a proper assessment of the needs of the class. These can never be determined solely by the age or experience or intelligence of the class. The needs of a particular group should soon be obvious. They may be concerned with spacing, footwork, confidence on apparatus, or the need to work in pairs or groups. There is no rule about the order of work except the teacher's assessment of the present needs of a particular class. Every class is different and has varying needs at different times. Occasionally it may be necessary to abandon work altogether and take a completely different kind of lesson if the mood and situation demands this. Flexibility in teaching is essential and easy to apply in physical education which, unlike other subjects, does not have to meet the demands of the examination syllabus.

HIERARCHY OF THEMES

Movement themes assume a hierarchical structure in that as each theme is worked it is absorbed and included in the next. Like the formation of concepts in thinking, each new experience adds to and changes the scheme or patterning in the mind/body action complex. As movements are repeated and used again and again in a variety of contexts, skill is built up and refined, understood and stored ready for immediate retrieval and use.

It has already been suggested that movement is so complex that the inter-relationship of thematic material is indivisibly locked. In theory a teacher could begin with any theme and work his way through a selection from the different groups and arrive at a similar result. A closer look shows that although there can be no set of rules or order of themes, some are simpler in concept and realisation than others.

In the early stages, movement themes evolve from the 'natural' movement of the children, such as running, jumping, swerving, tumbling, falling and so on. As skill and control begin to be evident, themes such as balance, flight, shape and partner relationships will clarify and define the area of work. Further refinement is demanded by focus on themes concerned with space, time and tension factors. These factors demand subtle definitions of changes of speed, changes of tension and the flow and flux of dynamic change of shape, accent and climax.

Each teacher will construct a hierarchy of themes for each of his classes. It is suggested that the following grouping might be helpful.

Introductory themes

      Travelling and stopping (locomotion)
      Weight-bearing
      Transference of weight
      Use of legs and feet
      Changes of speed

Intermediate themes

      Use of body surfaces in rolling, etc.
      Flight
      Balance and overbalance
      Twisting and turning
      Rising and falling
      Use of hands and arms
      Body shape
      Levels and directions
      Partner work

Advanced themes

      Swinging
      Symmetry and asymmetry
      Relationship of hands and feet
      Rhythmic patterns
      Tension and release
      Work in small and large groups

Those grouped under the heading Introductory Themes have different focal points. Some are action themes, and one is based on dynamics. The reasons for the choice of the action themes is obvious—they are basic to all movement. Many teachers begin with a theme on body shape, which is here placed in the second group. Experience shows that the work tends to become very static ("writhing and posing all over the apparatus" has been said) unless themes involving going and stopping are taken first. These themes are so also chosen as they lead to the body control needed for safety in negotiating apparatus. The theme on feet and legs included in this list results from the experience of dealing with inexperienced and untrained movers. People are so accustomed to their feet conveying them about that they treat them carelessly and roughly. In contrast, they treat their hands with care, placing them gently on the ground when preparing to take weight on them. This does not happen with their feet and almost immediately it is necessary to concentrate on their use. Dynamically the theme of change of speed is highlighted early on. It is an easy concept for children to understand and pleasurable to experience. The quick movements introduce the aspect of rhythm and climax and the slow movement helps the general body control.

Themes in the intermediate group concentrate on body parts, refining and clarifying the action and introducing more challenging and dangerous work. The themes on levels and directions increase variety of work and encourage a different 'look' at the same situations. They involve the aspect of the relationship of the pupil to spatial requirements and cues, and his mind must attend to the structure of the environment rather than to what his body is doing.

Themes in the advanced group are for pupils and students skilled in movement. They further refine bodily movement and make heavy physical and aesthetic demands. Some of them are particularly geared to demonstration purposes and can only be satisfactorily used by skilled and mature students. Each theme will be discussed in detail later in the book.

4 ANALYSIS OF A THEME

It is proposed to analyse a hypothetical theme under the following headings:

NAME OF THEME   CLASSIFICATION
GROUP

REASONS FOR SELECTION
DEFINITION
AIMS
OBJECTIVES
MOVEMENT MATERIAL   I.   EXPLORATION
II. DEVELOPMENT
III. REALISATION OF OBJECTIVES

This model will be used in analysing all the themes in this book. As each theme is worked it will be seen that not all sections and subdivisions will be relevant to each theme. The teacher should continually make selections relevant to his class and situation, and to his chosen theme, from the material suggested here. The classification and grouping of themes have been explained in Chapter 3.

SELECTION OF THEME

The teacher will select his theme according to his assessment of the immediate needs of a particular class or situation. It may be that the class is new to the school and the first task of the teacher will be to familiarise the children with the new space and apparatus. Some movement training involving landing, rolling and falling to ensure safety on apparatus will be needed to achieve this aim.

If on the other hand the teacher is new to the school, he may have to make contact with the children and establish confidence in them. In this case it may not be the right thing to immediately embark on a scheme of

25

work to improve the standard of performance. In one case a new teacher experienced difficulty in persuading a group of adolescent girls to make any real effort. The problem was solved by taking a series of lessons involving activities of partners and small groups. The girls gained confidence by helping each other, whereas they had been feeling awkward and conspicuous when asked to work on individual activities. The theme was used here to establish confidence and not because the girls were sufficiently skilled to develop their work into partner and group situations.

Another possibility is that the teacher is confronted with an energetic and able class whose consistent and outstanding fault is an untidy and careless use of their feet. A theme on use of feet and legs would be appropriate here. Again it is possible to meet a class of very good performers in the gymnasium who tend to move in straight lines and in only one direction, forwards. Here a theme on changes of direction could be developed. In some schools children have only worked on individual skills. In this situation the work could be extended by developing themes on the ways of working with a partner to evolve new patterns of movement and new possibilities of flight and support.

Only the teacher can decide what is appropriate to teach given the dynamic interchange of the set of relationships involving himself, the children, the particular space and equipment and the ideological framework of the school and department where he works. However, when he does settle on a theme his first task is to clarify the area of work.

DEFINITION OF THE THEME

The teacher must be clear in his own mind what material he is going to cover under the heading of a particular theme. He should know what has already been absorbed and where in the hierarchy of themes his choice lies. Although in his teaching he may exclude some possible aspects of the theme, he should include them in his definition. He should be aware where the limits of the theme fall and yet know the full extent of it. To this end he should list his aims, objectives and movement material.

AIMS OF THE THEME

The aims of the theme are to bring about certain changes in the understanding and behaviour of the children in the class. These may be concerned with the social aims of creating an atmosphere of discipline or a climate of learning, or of developing co-operative effort between members of the group. They may be concerned with development of a new gymnastic concept such as **balance** or **flight.** The theme could involve a bodily aim such as improvement in the awareness of **body shape,** or a more specific aim of practising the skill of bearing the **body weight** over the hands. Whatever the aim it should be possible to state it and detail a series of objectives which will achieve such aims.

OBJECTIVES OF THE THEME

The objectives of the theme will require the creation and perfection of pieces of work which arise from a series of set tasks in connection with the theme. Finished work will take the form of several sequences selected from the list below:

1. **Individual floor sequence**

   A sequence which requires the child to create a pattern of movement based on set tasks concerned with the theme using no apparatus and no partner help.

2. **Individual sequence using forms and mats**

   The use of forms and mats extends the range of movements possible in the previous sequence by adding a higher surface, a soft landing area and possibly stepped levels in the working area. In contrast to the large working space available in the individual floor sequence, the mats and benches setting (see p. 36) contains the action within a restricted area. This restriction forces frequent changes of direction and turning/twisting movements.

3. **Partner sequences**

   The co-operation of a partner again extends the range of movement possible by the use of support and further patterning possibilities, both matching and in contrast. (For more examples see p. 32-5). Partner sequences can be developed on the floor and on intermediate and large apparatus.

4. **Sequences on large apparatus**

   The large apparatus will yet further extend the development of the theme. The setting will highlight different aspects of the theme adding the further variables of height, angled surfaces, poles, bars and unstable apparatus, such as ropes. The teacher will allow the children a choice of work on apparatus, setting tasks at some pieces and finally asking for one or more finished sequences.

All these sequences will be in answer to specific tasks set by the teacher in connection with the movement material included in the theme. It is in the translating of the objectives into movement tasks that the area of movement material is defined.

MOVEMENT MATERIAL

The teacher, looking at his definition, his aims and objectives of the theme, must now clarify the movement material involved. If the theme is classified as an action theme it will have basic elements such as:

(i) the preparation for the action
(ii) the action itself
(iii) the recovery from the action

The basic elements involved in a theme on awareness of body parts will include:

(i) the range of movement possible to the part
(ii) the possibilities of the part supporting the weight of the body
(iii) use of the part in travelling
(iv) the use of the part in initiating actions such as swinging, turning, levering, etc.
(v) the use of the part in gesture and counterbalance
(vi) the use of the part in body shape

If the theme is one focusing on dynamics, such as changes of speed, suddenness and sustainment, the elements will be explored:

(i) in action
(ii) in combination with tension, in thrust, grip, resilience and other spatio/dynamic combinations
(iii) in the building of sequences of movement

The movement material is analysed into elements and then explored and developed. The children are required to select from the material and compose sequences of movement which will realise the objectives of the theme.

MOVEMENT MATERIAL I   EXPLORATION OF THEME

To explore means to seek, to find out, to range over for the purpose of discovery, to search. This is exactly what the teacher encourages his class to do when he introduces a new movement theme. He wants them to search out and range over every possible connection and tributary of the theme before the territory can be thoroughly known. In relation to the chosen theme the teacher encourages the children to range over a selection of movement material drawn from ideas suggested under the following headings:

1. Action of the whole body

The flow of movement of the body can be analysed into a series of gross body actions. In gymnastics these actions can be listed under several headings such as travelling, jumping and balancing actions, twisting and turning actions, actions involving contraction and extension of the body. Travelling actions include stepping and rolling actions. Stepping actions involve the transfer of body weight from one part to another, these parts usually being non-adjacent to each other. Examples of stepping actions are, moving from one foot to another or from hands to feet, or head to knees. Rolling actions transfer the weight from one part to adjacent parts and include falling and rocking actions. Jumping actions involve the ejection of the body into the air and have three phases, the take-off, the flight path and the recovery. The take-off may be made from various body parts, the flight position may be completely airborne or partly supported and the recovery achieved by a balanced landing or an off-balance fall or roll. Balance implies inaction rather than action, the achievement of a poised equilibrium over a small base, but the balance also has a variety of preparatory and recovery movements. The body can turn on its axes, which are vertical, as in a spin, or horizontal (s. to s.) as in a forward roll or horizontal (f. to b.) as in a cartwheel (see p. 129) A twist occurs when one part of the body is fixed while the rest turns, or where parts of the body turn in different directions. Contraction of the body occurs when all parts are drawn together round a particular part which may be one side, one foot or even the head (in a head-stand). Extension occurs when all parts of the body spread away from the centre and radiate from it in different dimensions.

The first method of exploration is to vary the body action, or to combine one or more gross bodily actions which can then be performed at the same time. For example, a balance can include an extension of the body, a jump can combine with a turn, or a stepping action with a twist.

2. Use of separate body parts

(i) As a base to take weight

The second method of variation may be by *changing the body part(s) supporting the body weight.* The weight is usually supported and carried about by the feet but it may also be taken by the hands, the head, shoulders, knees and many other parts or combination of parts. As the body is supported on particular parts it is helped and balanced by the counterbalancing action or gesture of other parts. For example, a position of balance on one shoulder can only be maintained by the counter-balancing spread of arms and legs.

(ii) To initiate action

A change of weight or action may be initiated by separate body parts, for example, the swing of a leg may lever the body into an inverted position or the swing of the arms may set a turning action in motion. The same action may be varied by changing the body part which initiates it. For example, a balance on hands may resolve into standing by the arms bending and the body rolling forwards, or by the legs swinging over into a crab position, or by the waist twisting and contracting so that the feet land to the side of the hands.

Thus the first and second methods of exploration may be listed as follows:

Variation in use of the body
Combination of body actions
Change of body part supporting weight
Change of body part initiating action
Use of different parts as levers or counter-balancing agents

3. Exploration of time, force and space

(i) The most important element to explore is that of space

All the actions of the body described above may be varied according to the spatial content used by the mover. This spatial content includes movement in the kinesphere, that is the area into which the parts of the body can extend without travelling. It also includes the area into which the body can travel in a given enclosure both on the ground, over apparatus and into the air.

Movements in the *kinesphere* may be classified according to the *levels and directions* into which it is possible to contract, extend, twist, without moving the base.

In actions such as travelling, leaping, balancing, falling, the gymnast may also move within his own kinesphere. He, as it were, transports his kinesphere with him as he goes. He may use a variety of floor patterns; curved, straight, twisted and zig-zag. He may use considerable variety in angles of approach to fixed apparatus. He may be required sometimes to limit the movement to a small space such as moving through an opening in a climbing frame, or the practise of recovering from flight in a confined area. At other times the sense of huge space which encourages freedom of movement may be experienced. The use of apparatus is a help to the development of spatial awareness with its possibilities of creating small, large and angled platforms and openings. It provides opportunities for height and the experience of going over, under, round, through, between a variety of obstacles which may be both stable or unstable. Exciting and interesting pathways, including drops, gaps and swings can be created. The space between the apparatus can be as important as the units themselves in suggesting pathways and floor patterns and flight paths through the air.

The exploration of the spatial element of movement therefore includes the movement of the body in many directions and levels both when it is still and in locomotion over the floor, apparatus or in the air. These ideas are used in conjunction with those concerning body action so that many permutations can be conceived and experienced. The body movements can be clarified by determining first, the main action, secondly, the use of particular body parts, and, thirdly, the exact direction and level of the pathway. A particular action can be varied by exploration of a variety of directions and levels and pathways before a final situation is created for practice and skilled performance.

(ii) Movements may be further refined and varied by **clarifying the dynamic content.** This refers to the *changing speeds and tensions* which enhance the flux and flow of movement patterns and are responsible for the accent, phrasing and rhythmic quality of movement. For example a movement pattern may be performed at top speed or very slowly. It can be varied so that some parts are very fast and some are slow, and then the experience reversed so that the fast movements are taken slowly and so on. Contrasts of speed, acceleration and deceleration and stillness add a new dimension to the performance of movement patterns and again add another varying factor to the exploratory section of the development of the work. For example, it is possible to move into a balance by a quick explosive action, or by a slow leverage, and this may be followed by a contrasting speed in the next action. Thus rhythmic phrases can be built up with accents and climaxes which may come at various times in a movement sequence.

(iii) **Changes in tension** also add variety to the work. Certain movements in themselves determine the amount of tension to be used, for example, a high leap demands a great deal of tension and force in the thrusting leg. In the same way the legs must use a controlled increase of tension as the body weight arrives back on the floor. But often a variety of tension can be used to heighten the dramatic interplay of movements in a sequence, for example, a series of jumps could be performed in a light, rhythmic, bouncy fashion or with the exciting power of maximum tension to achieve height and in the held flight position. Another example is of flight to land in a balance which could be held with slight tension in a poised position or

which could be held with strength and power, emphasising the contrast of
the absolute stillness and the fluency of the flight.

MOVEMENT MATERIAL II   DEVELOPMENT OF THEME

So far exploration of material has been discussed only in relation to the
individual and his own movement and the floor space.

1. Partner work

The range of possibilities can be increased still further by the introduction of *one or more partners.* This idea opens up many possibilities of
creating and experiencing movement which are not possible for the person
on his own, and which may cause him to adapt and adjust his ideas.

(i) One idea for using a partner consists in *using him as a piece of
apparatus* to move over, under, round, through. Once placed, a piece of
gymnastic apparatus stays still but a human body can change shape, make
an arch or a bridge, a platform or a spring-board, all within the same
sequence of action. This active apparatus causes the mover to change
direction and body shape and to respond to a constantly changing situation.

The partners can play with a variety of movement ideas, the one having
to respond as the other determines a change of activity by changing his
body position and shape. As the partners change role they have the
experience of alternately leading and then responding to each other's ideas.
This is a movement game in which the main idea is quick improvisation and
creation of new ideas.

(ii) There are several other ways of partners leading and adapting to
each other. These ideas include *copying a partner's sequence* in a mirroring
or follow-my-leader type situation. In this instance partner B learns to
reproduce exactly the work of partner A, and to perform the sequence so
that it matches exactly in action, timing and spatial patterning. Both
partners may have to make adjustments here as each begins to realise the
abilities and limitations of the other. Partner A may have to simplify his
sequence and partner B may have to work at unfamiliar movements so that
the two may achieve the task, which is to perfectly perform an identical
matching movement sequence.

(iii) Other ideas involve the adaptations which must be made if the
partners are required to share the same floor space or apparatus setting,
while continuing to move at the same time. This task requires constant
changes of direction and speed to make the best use of the available space,

at the same time avoiding another moving object, the body of the partner. Sequences based on this task can include exciting partner ideas such as following, chasing and near-miss collisions and so on. The more people that are sharing the same space the more intricate the situation becomes, demanding a sense of timing, a flexibility of body and pathway and a capacity for quick reaction and organisation of responses.

(iv) It is possible also for two or more people to work together with the central idea being that of *creating a visually exciting design.* Here it is the patterns of shapes that become important in the movement and these may be matching or contrasting. Possibly two or more bodies may interact to create one changing shape, or patterns in lines, circles or groups can be explored. For example, sequences of two or three people using progressive movement patterns upwards, sideways or diagonally on a window ladder can be very effective. The same idea can be extended to a rhythmic pattern, so that two, a group, or even a whole class can be working on different movements but within the same timing.

(v) So far none of these movement ideas has been concerned with contact with the body of a partner. *Counter-balancing partner's weight* provides opportunities to explore new movement possibilities in that the mover will have help and support from his partner. Before any exciting work can be achieved the partners must have some idea of the effort and control needed to even partially support another body. This can be gained by simple movements involving leaning towards each other and pushing back to an upright position, helping partner to lift and lower, swaying away from and moving towards partner. In these situations the partners would overbalance if it were not for the controlling effect of the partner's weight which is counter-balancing effectively. The partners can then experiment with different arm, wrist and hand grips and such movements as lowering the partner to the floor or assisting a partner into a difficult balance position. Partners can also control another's weight by using other parts of the body such as the back, hips, legs or feet, to partially support falling or balancing actions. A great deal of controlled muscular tension together with the use of one's own body-weight is necessary for both the partners, one to become an effective support and the other to be effectively supported. This kind of activity increases the pupil's knowledge of the body weight and strength of his own body and that of others. More than that, it makes him aware of the serious responsibility involved when another person is dependent on him for both safety and confidence.

(vi) The next stage of development is for *one partner to completely support the body of his partner.* There are many different parts of the body which can be gripped and used as supports. It is the function of the support to maintain a strong position so that the mover can rely on the steadiness of the body surface he is gripping, which may be the back, the knees and shoulders or hands and feet. In order to effectively lift a partner's weight the support must have his centre of gravity under that of his partner. Both partners should realise that effective lifting can only be achieved by the support being in a position to push or thrust upwards—this implies that the aim of the mover is to travel, fly or balance over the top of the partner.

This is particularly important where the supporting partner is to assist at the take-off of a mover attempting flight. Timing is very important here. For example, in a leapfrog, the support may add to the flight of the partner by lifting his back at the exact moment that the mover pushes off. This idea can be explored in many ways. The support can make a low or high back for the mover to use as a spring-board, or to vault over or round. The human apparatus improves on the static gymnastic apparatus by being able to boost the 'lift' or 'thrust' at the right moment just as the mover travels over.

The support may use other body parts such as hands and shoulders, or hands and feet for this purpose of being a dynamic piece of apparatus. Again the mover must hold a firm body position so that the supporter can lift him as it is impossible to lift a flaccid and relaxed body. The mover will also have to recover from considerable height and speed, probably without assistance, although it is possible for further help and support to be given during the recovery part of the movement. As the mover is coming down to the floor the support may assist by various hand grips or linking of arms to slow down the movement, absorb the momentum or correct the body position of the mover.

(vii) The last partner idea in this group is that of *swinging or carrying a partner.* In this idea the support is in control of the mover for a longer time and is concerned both with the grip and release of the mover. He is responsible for the safety of the partner as he travels or turns with him and for releasing him so that his recovery is safe. Again the grips can be varied and applied to different body parts so that a variety of ideas can be explored (see pp 33, 150). This idea is more often used in group situations where two or more people are concerned with the lifting and carrying and placing of another person. The 'body' can be also lifted onto and off apparatus, using a variety of flying and balancing actions and positions.

2. Introduction of intermediate apparatus

The second major way of developing the *theme* is by the introduction of apparatus. *Intermediate apparatus,* that is benches, mats, low surface areas and mattresses, is introduced first. It is used as a bridging experience between the floor work and the work on the large apparatus setting which is

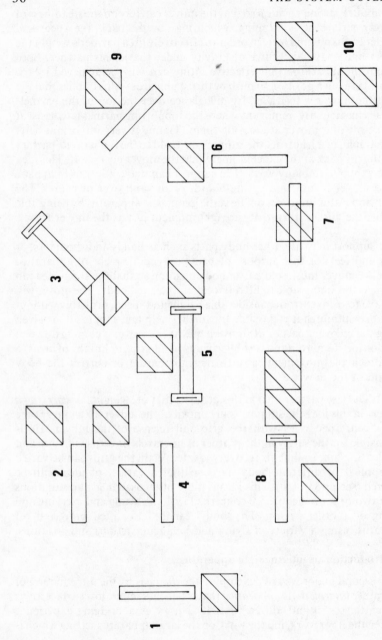

Fig. 3 Example of arrangement of intermediate apparatus.

to be used in connection with the particular theme. Benches and low areas, such as boxtops, provide raised or tilted areas for balance or take-off. They provide useful low platforms for tipping into a variety of recovery actions in preparation for possible drops and falls from higher apparatus later in the lesson. Mats and mattresses protect the large flat landing areas and invite falling and rolling actions that could be unsafe if tried on the floor. Any or all the exploratory ideas mentioned so far may be used on the intermediate apparatus setting, whose design and placing will create a new environment. This may both limit and extend the movement possibilities inherent in the ideas and tasks which have been already experienced at floor level.

Mats and forms and other low, stable apparatus should be arranged with care. Each individual setting should include space for take-off, balancing surface and landing area. Yet each one should be different. The angles at which forms and mats may be set should be varied, inviting many different directions, levels and angles of approach.

The mats may be placed in relationship to the form—either near to or far from it, at various angles to it or on top of it. In each intermediate setting there should be ten or more different arrangements for children to explore and to then use in the development of their ideas based on the theme. This setting will provide steps, slides, hills, gaps, angles and large and small recovery spaces, and in negotiating these the pupils will have to exercise more care and skill than they did on the floor.

The placing of mats and forms also confines the area of work spatially. Instead of the unlimited travelling areas provided by the floor, the gymnast must now confine himself to a limited area. This requires tighter turning actions to keep the flow of movement within the given area but at the same time, as the floor area is limited, the upward space can be extended by use of the apparatus.

Example of arrangement of intermediate apparatus (fig. 3; p. 36)

1 Reversed form: mat at end.
2 Form: two mats to right and left at one end of form.
3 Form inclined on to trestle: mat at lower end.
4 Form: mat to one side.
5 Form raised on two trestles: mats at one side and one end.
6 Form: mat at one end.
7 Form: mat over the top.
8 Form inclined onto trestle: two mats at high end, one mat to one side.
9 Form: mat at angle, to one side.
10 Parallel forms: mat at end: mat to one side.

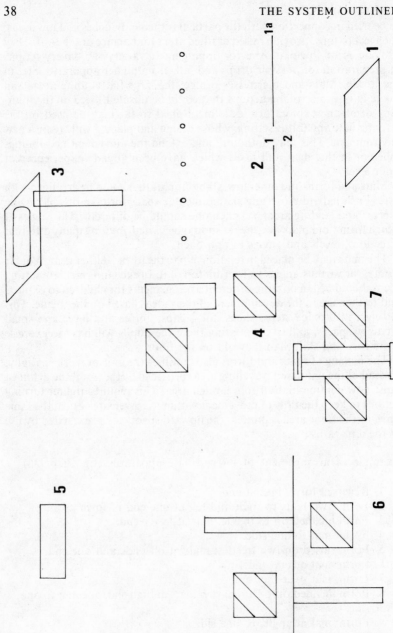

Fig. 4. Apparatus layout for weight-bearing theme.

3. Use of large apparatus (fig 4; p. 38)

It is the work on *large apparatus* which is tne most important part of the theme.

Large apparatus itself provides many new experiences for the students. Ropes and rope ladders are unstable and may swing and turn. It requires considerable effort just to cling onto them even before any movement or action task is attempted. Boxes, horses and vaulting tables provide strong, stable, comfortable surfaces at different heights and of varying shapes and sizes; bars and poles can be placed at different heights and angles and can be used to create narrow or wide openings. They can be gripped with different parts of the body, balanced on, swung round, climbed up or along or jumped through. Frames again provide small and large openings in a vertical, horizontal or angled plane. The trampettes and spring-boards are used to help the body overcome gravity and fly into the air and are very exciting for students to use. These ejective pieces of apparatus should be used with great care and the conditions in which people work on them should be closely controlled by the teacher (see p. 64, 113).

Large apparatus settings are chosen with the theme in mind.

There may be six or seven apparatus groups in any one class and each group should be working on a different aspect of the theme. For example, if weight bearing is the theme the following apparatus settings could be used.

1. Frame. Set at an angle.
   Task. Travel up the frame in an oblique direction taking weight on hands, feet and seat.

2. Ropes and bars. Bars set at three different heights.
   Task. a) Support weight in both upright and inverted position using hands and feet. Use ropes while still and while swinging.
   b) Explore ways of travelling along bars, balancing on them and hanging from them.

3. Horizontal frame, horse under, inclined form to frame.
   Task. Move under and over horse, frame, form, balancing on and hanging from different parts of the body.

4. Box: two mats as shown.
   Task. Arrive on box with weight on one body part, transfer it to another body part, spring onto mat.

5. Box horse.
   Task. Run, arrive on box on different body part(s) each time—transfer weight to hands and arrive on floor on feet.

6. Inclined forms onto bar (waist height): mats as shown.

Task. Move up forms with weight on same body part(s)—arrive on mats with hands touching first.

7. Forms on trestles of different heights: mats as shown.
   Task. Explore support of body weight shared between two body parts at different heights.

These settings emphasise the different parts of the body which can support or suspend the body weight. They give experiences of weight bearing in still and moving, stable and unstable, situations. Besides emphasising the theme opportunity should be given just to enjoy or explore each new setting. It is very frustrating to be confronted with exciting looking apparatus and not allowed to 'have a go' and just do what one likes for a short time. The apparatus should be exciting and challenging to dynamic action demanding courage as well as ingenuity from the students. When these factors have been considered and the class has had time to explore the tasks connected with the theme should be emphasised.

MOVEMENT MATERIAL III   REALISATION OF OBJECTIVES

It is with the formation of sequences that the work of the theme is completed. So far in this chapter ideas for exploration and development of movement ideas have been put forward. Now the final pieces of work must be chosen and perfected. Each theme results in several finished pieces of work which take the form of sequences of movement. There will probably be at least five sequences connected to each theme; one entirely concerned with work on the floor with no apparatus and no partner. There will also be individual sequences using intermediate and large apparatus. There may also be partner or group sequences, which may involve intermediate or large apparatus. These sequences will be based on tasks set by the teacher.

For example, the objectives of a theme on *weight-bearing* (see also p. 84) could be:

1.   An individual floor sequence showing the holding of body-weight over three different body parts during the sequence.

2.   A partner sequence in which partners help each other to take weight on small parts of the body, each partner using at least one inverted position.

3.   Mats and Forms. An individual sequence in which the weight of the body is taken on the form three times using a different area or part of the body each time. The mats should be used for the appropriate recoveries.

4/5. Select the set tasks at two different large apparatus settings and perfect them.

Creating sequences

The theme suggests certain inbuilt physical tasks. The theme of weight-bearing requires the children to experience the supporting of their body weight on many different body parts. Humans are accustomed to keeping their weight on their feet as when they stand or walk, or on their feet and seat as in sitting, or distributing it throughout their body as in lying. In gymnastics the weight is taken on many unusual body parts such as the hands, the head, the shoulders or one knee and one hand. During the working of the theme on weight-bearing the students explore all possible parts of the body which can support their weight. During the *exploration* they discover various ways of moving in and out of weight-bearing situations, and of transitions between one position and the next.

The building up of sequences is a slow process. The first stage is a *selection,* made by the child, from movements discovered during the exploratory material suggested by the teacher. The child may be helped and guided in his choice according to the judgement of the teacher. Having selected his actions he must try *linking them together.* This may take time and considerable experimentation in order to arrive at the most appropriate and harmonious movements. Again the child may need guidance in selecting the best transitions from one movement to another, as the end of one action blends into or becomes the beginning of the next. Once the movement pattern has been determined the *starting and ending of the sequence* will need attention. There should always be a clear and controlled body position at the beginning and ending of each sequence.

After the sequence is complete the overall 'look' and 'feel' of the work may need some improving. The climax of the sequence, the rhythmic pattern, possible changes of speed, direction and level should be emphasised. The sequence will need *much practise* and should be done over and over again until it is as nearly perfect as it can be. Children should show each other their finished work and be given criteria of judgement. These criteria could include the fidelity to the task, the originality of the answering movements, the transitions, the standard of performance and the demands in bodily skill and strength. All these criteria are equally important in achieving a sequence that is interesting and exciting to look at as well as to perform.

Once achieved, sequences of movement should not be forgotten put practised again at the beginning and end of future lessons. In this way the child gradually builds up her own vocabulary of skills and always has some work she can show, in the same way that she has her essays, paintings and other classroom work. Many schools now have access to videotape recording equipment and some of the best work can be permanently recorded, giving children staff and parents the opportunity of seeing and assessing the work again.

5 EXAMPLE OF ANALYSIS OF A THEME—BALANCE AND OVERBALANCE

THEME: **Balance/Overbalance**   CLASSIFICATION: **Action**
                                          GROUP: **Intermediate**

SELECTION

This theme might be chosen for a class of children who are already competent in movement but who need a greater degree of control in their work. Themes already covered could have been concerned with travelling and stopping, weight-bearing, transference of weight, body shape, flight.

DEFINITION

This theme involves the experience of holding the body in stillness while decreasing the area of the weight-bearing surface as far as possible. Balance is experienced using different body surfaces and parts as load-bearing bases. The theme emphasises the tension required to adjust the body to a smaller weight-bearing surface and also the need for the limbs to act as counterbalancing agents.

It will include the various ways in which the body can achieve and lose balance, the use of a partner in increasing the possibilities of balance and the maintaining of balance in various stable and unstable apparatus situations.

AIMS

The aim of the theme is to clarify in the minds of the children the concept of balance both through understanding and experience. A variety of practices will be suggested to increase bodily knowledge of, and skill in, the technique of gaining, maintaining and losing balance.

OBJECTIVES

1.   An **individual floor sequence** to include the holding of the body in balance over three different bases. The shape of the body should be different in each balance.

2. **Mats and forms.** An individual sequence to include:
   a) a leap into a balance
   b) a roll into a balance
   c) a twist into a balance

3. A **partner sequence.** This may be on the floor, intermediate or large apparatus and each partner should be used:
   a) as a support in maintaining balance
   b) as a platform on which to balance

4/5. **Large apparatus.** Choose two apparatus settings on which to form sequences which will include:
   a) swinging on to apparatus into a still position
   b) leaping on to apparatus to hold a still position
   c) holding a still position on moving apparatus

MOVEMENT MATERIAL I   EXPLORATION OF THEME

1. **Balance on different body parts**
   Practise holding the body in balance over different bases, reducing the area of support while maintaining the stillness. The bases will be discovered by students in experimental situations, but will include:
   (i) Balance on small body parts. For example:
      a) Two feet—reduce to one foot
      b) Two hands—reduce to one hand
      c) Two feet, one hand—reduce to one foot, one hand
      d) Two hands, one knee—reduce to one hand, one knee
      e) Two hands and head—reduce to one hand and head
   (ii) Balance on large body areas such as:
      a) Shoulders—reduce to one shoulder
      b) Hips—reduce to one hip
      c) Tummy—reduce to front of hips (on bench or bar)
   The child will discover many others, see picture p. 83.

2. **Vary the shape of the body in balance**
   While the body is being held in stillness over a given base, e.g. the head and hands, the body shape may be varied. It may be:
   (i) Contracted round a given part which may be
      a) Tummy
      b) One side
      c) One corner of body area
      d) Back
   (ii) Extended
      a) In a long thin shape
      b) In a wide shape using two or three dimensions

   (iii) Part extended, part contracted
   (iv) Twisted
   (v) Symmetrical body shapes
     a) both sides of body matching
     b) upper and lower halves alike
    Asymmetrical
     a) both sides different
     b) both halves different

3. **Achieve balance by:**
   (i) Swinging into balance, such as:
     a) Swing one leg to arrive in balance on hands
     b) Swing both legs to arrive in balance on head
     c) Use of apparatus to assist swing (ropes) to arrive on knees, seat, etc. on surface of box.
   (ii) Jumping into balance, for example:
     a) Onto one foot
     b) Into sitting (on apparatus)
     c) Onto shoulders (on apparatus)
     d) By use of apparatus to assist jump—trampette—beating board.
   (iii) Rolling into balance, for example:
     a) Forward roll into balance on one foot
     b) Backwards roll into balance on head, shoulder or hands
     c) Sideways roll into balance on one forearm and one knee or one shoulder, etc.
   (iv) Twisting into balance, for example:
     a) From another balanced position
     b) With a jump from a standing position
     c) With a swing from a height
   (v) Levering into balance, for example:
     a) Slow leverage of legs into headstand
     b) Slow leverage of legs into balance on shoulder.

4. **Recover from balance by:**
   (i) Deliberately moving centre of gravity (hips) so that a stepping action occurs:
     a) Balance on one foot tip body and catch weight on the other foot
     b) Balance on hands, tip body to land on feet, either sideways or 'crab' position
     c) Balance on one body part, tip to adjacent part e.g. knees to seat, seat to shoulders
     d) Balance on a body part, tip to take weight on non-adjacent part e.g. head to feet.
   (ii) Falling and rolling:
    Balance on one part of body, e.g. head, hands, knees, shoulder.

Throw centre of gravity away from base and catch weight by falling and/or rolling down front, back or side surfaces of the body.

(iii) Twisting the body until the centre of gravity is no longer over the base, for example:

Balance on shoulders, slowly twist waist until knees begin to tip weight over one shoulder, then transfer weight to knees. This can be tried from balance on many different body parts.

(iv) The action of the base itself, for example:
    a) springing off the feet
    b) pushing off hands
    c) springing off shoulders, seat, tummy (from apparatus).

MOVEMENT MATERIAL II   DEVELOPMENT OF THEME

1. **Partner work** (see also p. 122).
The partner may be used in the following ways:
  (i) As a platform on which to balance
  (ii) As a support; with assistance it is possible to hold balance positions that are impossible for the individual alone
  (iii) As a counter-balancing agent—the partner balances the weight of the other by the carefully controlled use of his own body weight
  (iv) To assist in the achieving of balance by lifting, gripping, swinging
  (v) To assist in the recovery from balance by controlling partners weight in coming off apparatus. Examples of these partner activities are given in illustrations on page 33.

2. **Intermediate apparatus.**
Using the setting of intermediate apparatus as illustrated and described on p. 36, selections from all the ideas given in movement material I and II should be made.

3. **Large apparatus.** (see p. 48 for diagram, explanation and tasks.)
Gymnastic apparatus provides a variety of platforms on which the body can perch, such as:
  (i) Flat surfaces of varying textures: leather, wood, plastic, metal, rubber
  (ii) Flat surfaces of varying sizes and shapes: round, square, oblong
  (iii) Flat surfaces at varying levels: high, low, stepped
  (iv) Sloping surfaces at various angles which may be wide, narrow or rounded (poles)
  (v) Swinging surfaces such as trapeze or rope ladder
  (vi) Vertical surfaces, poles
  (vii) Moving surfaces—box-horse on wheels.

The wording of the tasks together with the setting of the apparatus will suggest several ways of moving into and out of the various balanced positions.

MOVEMENT MATERIAL III   REALISATION OF OBJECTIVES

The objectives are stated on page 43-4.

THE MASTER PLAN OF THE THEME

The theme defined and analysed, points to units of work(see p. 2f Chapter I). The work units are selected by the teacher from the movement material related to the theme. Work units are organised into a MASTER PLAN which will provide lesson material for about five lessons. Some themes can stand longer treatment and others less. The master plan forms a pattern of tasks from which individual lessons can be composed: it consists of:

    I.   Ways of introducing the theme
    II. Exploration of the theme
    III. Developing the theme
    IV Forming sequences

The following model of a master plan for a theme has been found useful. The columns are used as a rough check and reminder—the ticks being inserted immediately after the lesson, before the teacher has had time to write his commentary. (see p. 49f).

In preparing each individual lesson the teacher makes a selection from this scheme choosing some tasks from each work unit. From this he makes his lesson plan. AFTER the lesson he ticks off the work he has achieved in the appropriate column. On this plan the work for the first two lessons has been indicated and it is ready for preparation of the third lesson. In this particular series of lessons it will be noted that the recovery actions are practised first. The first time apparatus is used, free exploration is allowed and the class is divided into groups only for the erection and dismantling of apparatus. It will also be noted that a good deal more movement is achieved in the second lesson than the first for two reasons. The first is that part of the work is repetition from the first lesson, and the second is that time is saved as the large apparatus is not used.

Each teacher will decide which selections to make from the model according to the particular situation he is in. There is no right and wrong about this. It is wise, nevertheless, to ensure that there is a variety of movement in each lesson which should include travelling, flight, inversion and variety of body shape.

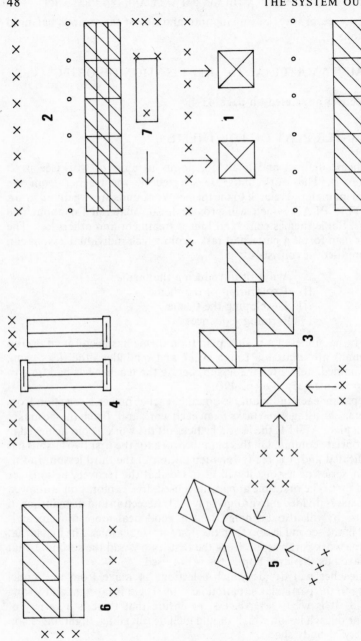

Fig. 5. Large apparatus Lay-out, x pupil's starting point.

EXAMPLE OF MASTER PLAN OF THEME—BALANCE AND OVERBALANCE

	C1	C2	C3	C4	C5	C6
I INTRODUCTION OF THEME						
(i) Running, stop in balance on						
feet						
hands	✓					
on other body parts	✓					
(ii) Practise ways of balance on hands		✓				
(iii) Revise rocking and rolling actions		✓				
II EXPLORATION OF THEME						
(i) Practise balance on different body						
parts, head, hand(s)	✓	✓				
and foot or feet	✓	✓				
other small parts	✓	✓				
parts of trunk	✓	✓				
(ii) Change body shape while in balanced position						
(iii) Practise falling from balance on						
shoulders into roll		✓				
knees into roll	✓	✓				
hips into into roll		✓				
other parts into roll		✓				
(iv) Practise twisting from balance on						
shoulders		✓				
hands		✓				
head		✓				
other parts		✓				
(v) Jumping into balance on						
feet						
hands						
(vi) Rolling into balance on						
shoulders						
head						
hands						
other parts						
(vii) Swing into balance						
hands						
head						
III 1. MATS AND FORMS						
(i) Balance on form, vary bases		✓				

(ii) Vary ways of recovering ✓

(iii) Vary ways of arriving in balance on form

(iv) Practise (i)—(iii) using different arrangements of forms and mats ✓

2. PARTNER WORK

(i) Find ways of balancing on partner

(ii) Find ways of helping partner to balance ✓

3. LARGE APPARATUS (See fig. 5)

(i) Two trampettes, ropes, mats
 a) Free exploration ✓
 b) Jump from trampettes to ropes and swing into inverted position, hold, drop to mats

(ii) Ropes, bars, mats under—bars hip and shoulder height
 a) Free exploration ✓
 b) Swing onto bar, move into balance, twist off to land on mat

(iii) Trampette or springboard, boxes at right-angles, three mats
 a) Free exploration ✓
 b) Use trampette to arrive in balance on box, change to balance on another body part, arrive on mats hands first

(iv) One inclined reversed form, one raised reversed form, mats
 a) Free exploration ✓
 b) Walk along forms, forward, backward, sideways, mats for practising, balancing and falling

(v) Horse, two mats
 a) Free exploration ✓
 b) Run, leap onto horse, arrive in balance on hands, feet, knees or seat; push off

(vi) 'Carco' benches, stepped, one shoulder height, one waist height, mattress as shown

    a) Free exploration
    b) Discover ways into and out of balancing on stepped area
(vii) Box horse—pushed by two people
    a) Hold balance position, whilst apparatus in motion

IV SEQUENCES

As in detailed theme
  (iv) Individual sequence (floor)
  (ii) Individual sequence (mats and forms)
  (iii) Partner sequence
  (iv) Apparatus sequence a)
                         b)

V CLOSING MOVEMENTS

  (i) Performance of individual floor sequence
  (ii) Copy sequence of slow balances set by teacher
  (iii) Stand still—heels lift—balance on toes, holding head high—heels lower to good standing position
     Walk slowly to changing rooms

After each lesson a commentary should be written. Very often the lesson does not follow the plan of the teacher. Children introduce new ideas and it is often wise to follow these up. Lesson plans are not there to be slavishly followed, but are there as safe-guards. They ensure that there will be a well-constructed lesson which has been carefully considered both in the choice of material and in the organisation for speed and safety reasons. Planning does not kill spontaneity unless it is followed with inflexible devotion. Spontaneity cannot arise in a vacuum nor can students create out of nothing. Experiences, environments, suggestions and open-ended tasks help to spark off the desire to work and experiment with ideas—but to be of real value these teaching strategies must not be random, but thoughtfully considered and carefully graded and structured. The lesson plan can even be abandoned if more interesting ideas arise in the lesson. In any case both the plan and the actual lesson will need careful evaluation when preparation for the next lesson is made.

It is suggested that INDIVIDUAL LESSONS could be organised in the following way:

|---|---|---|
| 52 | | THE SYSTEM OUTLINED |

Lesson I. Floor work, introduction of theme and explore 20 mins.
Apparatus (large), exploration 10 mins.

Lesson II. Floor work, explore and select 15 mins.
Intermediate apparatus, explore 15 mins.

Lesson III. Intermediate apparatus, explore and select 15 mins.
Large apparatus, explore and select 15 mins.

Lesson IV. Floor work, selection and practice 10 mins.
Large apparatus, selection and practice 20 mins.

Lesson V. Floor work, perfect sequence 10 mins.
Intermediate apparatus, perfect sequence 10 mins.
Large apparatus, perfect sequence 10 mins.

6 STRUCTURING INDIVIDUAL LESSON PLANS

At the end of the last chapter a breakdown of the work into a series of lessons was suggested. This series shows a build-up to a complete lesson of finished work, that is, the perfection of sequences based on the theme. The choice of basic sequence ideas is as follows:

Individual sequences on floor
Individual sequences on intermediate apparatus
Individual sequences on large apparatus
Partner or group sequences on floor and/or apparatus

So the last lesson of a series will consist of performance of work, individual and in pairs or groups, on the floor, on mats and forms and/or on large apparatus.

The whole range of this work cannot be included in each lesson if there is to be a time allocated to exploration, selection and coaching. The last lesson of a series may be the only one in which all parts of the theme are covered. In planning any individual lesson *its relationship to other lessons in the series* is the first consideration. For example, if large apparatus was not used in the last lesson it should feature in the present one, or, if no sequence has yet been attempted, most of the lesson may have to be spent on this. Generally speaking, in a given single period in a school timetable it is only possible to plan thirty minutes activity and, therefore, only two major areas of work can be covered. This may be floor work and intermediate apparatus, or it could be both intermediate and large apparatus, ignoring the floor work. Whichever is chosen depends on what has happened in the previous lesson and what is tentatively planned for the next.

Once the framework of the lesson is decided the material must be chosen. Although the material will be part of the ongoing theme it will be selected as a direct result of the teacher's evaluation of the previous lesson. He will consider the response of the children to the material in the last lesson and decide whether it was aptly chosen and correctly presented. He may decide

53

to repeat the material, or much of it, but to try a more appropriate method of teaching. Alternatively he may discard some of the work begun but develop the rest possibly adding new ideas. By and large, his aim will be to incorporate and build on that which has gone before and develop it along the lines he has planned. He should include some new ideas and work in order to leave growing points for future lessons.

He will also select his material so that it will make a *balanced lesson*. Basically the lesson is planned in two main parts, the first being a careful and deliberate preparation for the second. The experiences given in the first part of the lesson provide the material from which children may draw appropriate answers to the tasks set in the second part. The tasks in the second part of the lesson are structured towards the objectives set out in the theme and require the children to make decisions and choices and create short individual pieces of work. There is a build-up in the concentrated attention needed to answer more clearly defined tasks as the lesson progresses.

Besides being logical in its sequence the choice of material should provide a *balanced physical diet*. The lesson must provide opportunities for energetic exercise, flight, inversion, change of body shape and contrasts of tension and speeds. Children need exercise for strengthening and mobilising the whole body and care must be taken not to over use any one part. There should be a gradual increase in the physical demands the lesson makes as well as in the creative aspects of the lesson mentioned above.

The lesson *also develops socially* as it progresses. At the beginning the children work alone as they come into the gymnasium from the changing rooms. As the work progresses they may be asked to work in pairs on some movement task. As the lesson proceeds to the stage of intermediate apparatus the child must cooperate with two or three others to arrange the mats and forms. At the climax of the lesson, the large apparatus work, the children cooperate in groups to erect the equipment, work on it and dismantle it. Sometimes during the lesson, or at the end, the whole class may be asked to work as one large group. Thus in each lesson the child experiences several changes in relationship with members of the class and in mixed groups. The physical contact between the sexes in the context of the gymnasium has proved to be of great benefit to the group. They gain a new insight into the kind of responsibility they can take for each other and of each others' strengths and limitations. A new respect for each other has been noticed by teachers of mixed groups at secondary level; the boys adding excitement and vitality to the work and the girls having more awareness of extremes of quality in performance.

This development of material and social contact implies a corresponding *build-up in the organisation* of the lesson. The need for detailed planning of events becomes more urgent as the lesson proceeds. Successful handling of apparatus, for example, depends on pre-planning in several ways. The apparatus should be prepared at the beginning of the lesson and set in appropriate spaces in the gymnasium, ready to be carried into place later in the lesson. The order of setting up of pieces of apparatus must have been decided as well as the number of children that are needed to carry it. Neglect of any of these factors can cause chaos and lead to potentially dangerous situations.

The organisation of the children is an important responsibility. This begins in the changing room with the supervision of changing and collection of valuables, continues throughout the lesson and ends with the control of showering and dressing arrangements. During the lesson such factors as spacing of the children correctly for each activity is important, handing out specific responsibilities and checking and rechecking apparatus settings.

In the gymnasium the safety of the children is paramount—there cannot be too much attention given to this factor—see p. 64f.

The relationship between teacher and children is also important. After all this planning and organisation has been done, the teacher must think of the atmosphere he wishes to create and this will include a careful consideration of each task he sets and even the words he uses to clarify it. Slick organisation and economy in talk and explanations help to keep the lesson moving at a spanking pace and prevent irritation and boredom in children which can in turn lead to carelessness and potential danger. He will also think of possible reactions to his task and the teaching points which might be needed during the lesson and note these.

With these considerations in mind the teacher, master plan of theme before him, sets out to choose his lesson. First, he checks, via his columns of ticks and lesson commentaries, what the class has done. Memory alone is not a good guide. In a secondary school a teacher may be working forty-five periods a week and with many parallel groups, so the keeping of adequate records is essential. Then he works through the lesson keeping the following thoughts in mind:

1. The basic framework of lesson   –   floorwork
                                                      intermediate apparatus
                                                      large apparatus

2. Structure of lesson   –   opening activity
                                                      teaching material leading to
                                                      formation of sequences
                                                      closing activity

3. Details of work units   –   selection from several or all of
                                                      work units shown on master plan

4. Organisation of lesson   –   handling and placing of apparatus
                                       traffic of children

5. Wording of tasks and instructions

6. Consideration of teaching points, based on what the teacher expects to
   see as a result of his tasks and instructions.

An example of one way of setting out lesson plans is given below.

This lesson plan in made for the first lesson on master plan and
corresponds to the ticks.

ACTIVITY	ORGANIZATION	TEACHING
(Units of work)	(Apparatus, children)	
I Run-stop on different body parts.	Spacing Change of direction All commands quick and clear	(i) Run & stop - stop dead (ii) Run, stop on one foot - *stillness* (iii) Run, stop on toes - *stillness* (iv) Run, stop on shoulders (v) Run, stop on other parts (*stillness*)
(2-3 mins.)		
II. Balance on different body parts.	Individual work in own territory	(i) Take weight on shoulders, tip over and try to take weight on one shoulder.
	Free experiment with suggestions from teacher	(ii) Try other body parts - such as hands, head and hands, hands and foot, knee and hands. Reduce base each time. *Coach stillness and poise, point out need of body tension to hold balance.*
Falling from knees	" " "	(i) Take weight on knees, seat and shoulders
	Repeat movement on the other side.	(ii) Balance weight on knees, tip weight off balance on to seat and shoulders.

ACTIVITY	ORGANISATION	TEACHING
Take weight on hands by leg swing (10-12 mins.)	Individual space	*Coach stillness and slow tip followed by quick fall.* (i) Swing one leg up to take weight on hands (ii) Balance on hands as long as possible. (iii) Change legs (iv) Change pattern made by legs. *Coach hips over shoulders and stillness over base (hands).*
III. Explore large apparatus (15 mins.)	Form groups Place groups in appropriate spaces Go round groups, explain apparatus settings Check settings Free spacing Return to groups to dismantle	(i) Explore own apparatus when erected (ii) Free exploration of all apparatus (iii) Discover platforms where it is possible to balance. (iv) Discover areas for falling or rolling.
Standing, heel raising and lowering (1 min.)	Individual spaces Copy teacher's movement	*Stillness, poise, good posture.*

N.B. All teaching points are *italicised*, or may be written in a different colour.

Commentary on lesson

In this space write notes and comments relevant to this lesson as soon as possible after it takes place. Using these comments and the master plan, prepare the next lesson.

The teacher's notebook should contain:

1. A detailed theme for each group of classes working on a given theme.
2. A master plan for each class.
3. Lesson notes, in diary form, for each class.

7 USE OF APPARATUS

By definition the gymnasium is a room set aside for the training of the body. In British schools this room is expensively equipped with special wood floors and a variety of leather, metal and wooden apparatus. It is, in fact, one of the most expensive rooms in the building. It is rapidly becoming one of the least used.

This is certainly not due to lack of interest among the school population. Children anticipate the excitement of using the apparatus and look forward to their lessons. All too often they are disappointed for the apparatus is rarely used. Sometimes the lessons are too short and the teacher opts for some sort of circuit training in order to get maximum bodily exercise in the shortest possible time. Frequently lessons are cancelled for extra academic work or examinations or even as a punishment. Whatever the reason, in many schools the apparatus is not used.

It may be that the teachers themselves are lacking in confidence and familiarity with the apparatus, in spite of the fact that it has been provided both at school and at college. Many of those who do work with apparatus use only a few pieces and often in similar rather stereotyped arrangements which allow very little variety of movement. The apparatus is often set so that pathways are invariably straight, directions forwards and a small restricted recovery area allowed. All too often the organisation of apparatus handling is so bad that half the lesson is wasted in erection and dismantling, leaving very little time for use. If the children are then arranged in files so that they use the apparatus one after the other, the chances are that any one child in the class might touch the apparatus no more than two or three times per lesson.

Other problems arise out of children's lack of confidence when confronted with an apparatus setting. They do not know how to get on or over the apparatus, what to do on it or how to recover. More often than not they attempt ·to perform ,some feat they have seen done on television or elsewhere. If they fail, or hurt themselves, apprehension and uncertainty colour their attitude to any further attempts. It is fashionable in some schools today to allow free play with no explanation or help from the teacher. What then does a child do when he sees a trampette for the first time? Other schools insist that children work in groups at certain pieces of equipment and in this situation the child may easily find himself afraid of the apparatus at which he is placed.

From the very first lessons the children should be using apparatus confidently and happily. The skill of the teacher lies in establishing the climate of safety and control where this can happen. A great deal of time and thought should be given to apparatus arrangements to ensure that they are appropriate for the particular class. The teacher must cater for a variety of shapes, sizes, and abilities in each set of children. It is his aim to allow each child the maximum experience of which he is capable—even the clumsy child should have opportunity to work at his own level without feeling conspicuous.

CHOOSING APPARATUS

There are several basic considerations that the teacher may take into account when determining his large apparatus settings.

1. Routes on and off apparatus

Apparatus can be arranged so that there are opportunities in the settings for the most able child in the class as well as the most clumsy. This can be assured by making several routes of approach to the apparatus. For example, whereas some children can jump to reach a high bar, others may need the help of a box or a bench. Likewise there should be more than one way off a piece of apparatus; mats may be placed in the right position so that children may jump off, a rope could be just within reach for swinging away from apparatus, or poles and benches could be placed for sliding down from it.

2. Freedom of choice of apparatus

There should always be a choice of apparatus for the children. If children are allocated into groups there could be a choice of situations in the same group—two levels of platform could be provided, perhaps, or an alternative arrangement in the same area of the gymnasium. No child should ever feel impelled to go onto apparatus if he feels apprehensive.

3. Spacing of apparatus

It goes without saying that consideration should be given to the spacing of apparatus to ensure there is enough approach and recovery space. Other points that need watching are the height above the apparatus and its proximity to walls, doors, or other groups. In determining the layout it is unwise to have two sets of apparatus which demand similar kinds of bodily activity (e.g. hanging) close together. In the diagram below the child moves from (i) to (vi), no two similar body experiences are consecutive.

(i)	(iv)	(v)
(ii)	(iii)	(vi)

(i) hanging
(ii) jumping
(iii) inversion
(iv) heaving
(v) flight
(vi) part heave, part twist, part support

The apparatus itself demands certain types of bodily activity before any tasks are set and should emphasise the ideas the teacher wants to develop. For example, the spacing of the pieces of apparatus may suggest a variety of pathways or levels, size and shape of gaps or openings and angles of ascent and descent.

ORGANISATION OF THE CLASS

Deciding the layout of the apparatus is only the first of the teacher's problems. The next is to ensure the efficient organisation of the class.

1. Preparation of the gymnasium

Many gymnasia have small apparatus stores, some with doors. Chaos reigns in classes where 40 children descend in the apparatus store at once to get out their allotted pieces. Before the lesson the teacher should set out the main pieces of apparatus to be used in the gymnasium at easily accessible vantage points. Class monitors can be responsible for this task and teachers can prepare them for this by either pinning up a diagram in the classroom or cloakroom or keeping a blackboard for instructions in the gymnasium. The majority of the apparatus should be removed from the store at the beginning of the day and should stay out until after the last lesson when it should be returned to the safety of the store. Mats and benches should be stacked in at least four different places in the gymnasium so that time will

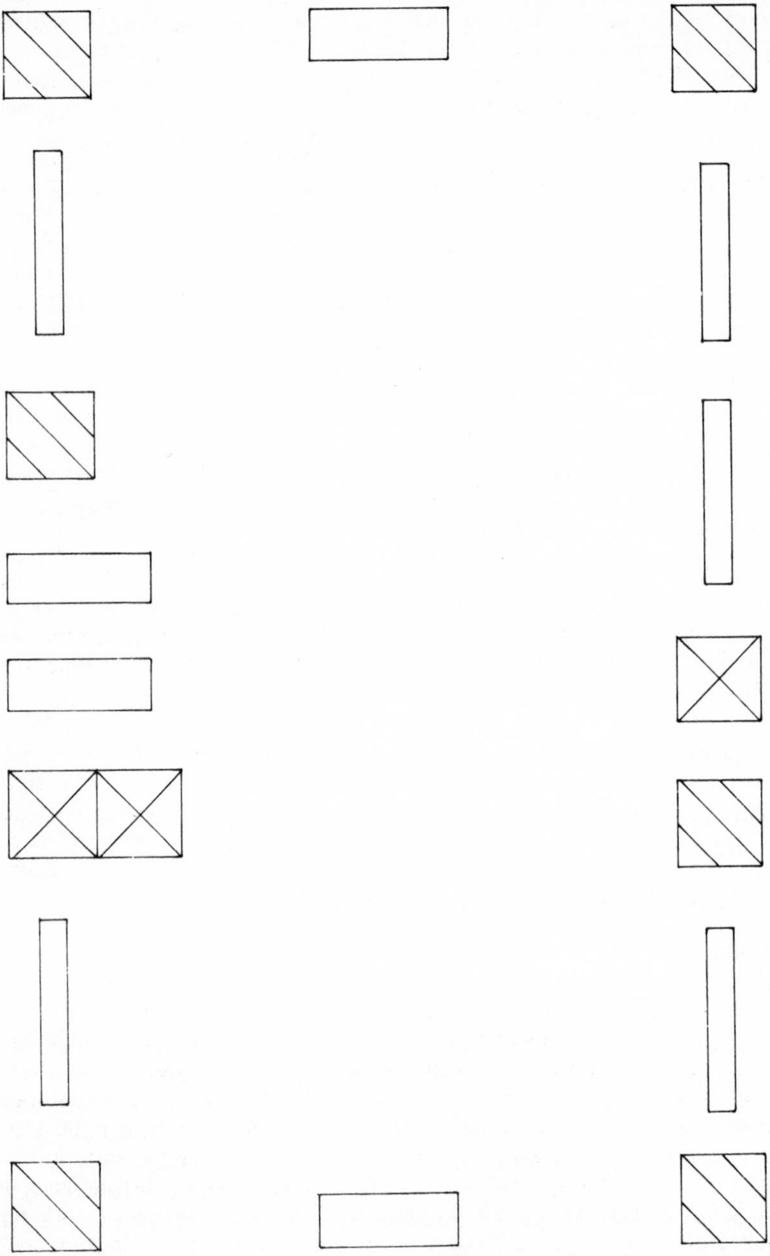

Fig. 6. Gymnasium prepared for lesson.

not be wasted by children queuing to get their apparatus from the same place.

2. Organisation of traffic

Again it is important for the teacher to organise the comings and goings of the children in very great detail. Apparatus should be lifted, carried and placed and not dragged, dropped and thrown. Habits concerning the numbers of children to carry each piece should be learned and strictly maintained. The order in which apparatus should be erected and dismantled should be clarified. A routine for getting out and checking fixed apparatus should be established. The whole business of apparatus handling is good for the education of children in co-operation and leadership. They take pride in efficiency and accuracy and a well-trained class can take almost full responsibility for this side of the work. Most teachers find that in each new apparatus setting it is wise to allocate a particular group of children to a particular setting—so that wherever they may be working in the gymnasium they are responsible for the getting out and putting away of their own pieces.

3. Noise level in the class

If a class is working hard and taking responsibility for apparatus it is silly to expect a strict silence. There should be a buzz of activity and the minimum of talk. In this situation, which is always one of potential danger, the teacher must be able to gain immediate silence and a cessation of activity should this become necessary. In the early stages the teacher and class must come to mutual understanding about signals and what they mean—which are urgent and need immediate response and which ask for a controlled slowing down and stopping of activity. There should be no noise of apparatus except the slotting of uprights of bars into position—every operation should be done with care and control.

WORK ON APPARATUS

The first problem that confronts the teacher is the method of establishing a real confidence in the class when they begin work on apparatus. A real confidence implies a sense of responsibility and an awareness of possible dangers. Many children and teachers are over confident and this is as worrying as a fear of using apparatus. This over confidence reveals itself in both children and teacher encouraging and attempting difficult and spectacular stunts instead of gradually allowing the children to feel their way around and over the apparatus. Teachers feel a need to 'teach' and sometimes suggest such dangerous actions to children that it is surprising that there are so few accidents in gymnasia today. Fortunately, young children rarely attempt activities which they cannot manage: even to please an enthusiastic teacher.

INTRODUCTION OF APPARATUS

Apparatus can be introduced to children in one of two ways. It can be introduced gradually, so that in the first lesson only mats and benches are used. In the second lesson mats, benches and boxes may be used. In the third lesson ropes may be added. In each lesson the children learn to handle or operate a new piece of equipment until all are familiar with every piece. This takes a great deal of time and care but pays dividends in later lessons.

The second way, routine in many of our primary schools, is for the older children or caretaker to erect all the apparatus so that the class enters a room full of apparatus to see a man-made jungle. At whatever age children first meet a gymnasium full of apparatus they find it stimulating and exciting. They long to be on it and should have the opportunity to do so at once. The following method of procedure relating to the second method of introduction, has proved to be useful.

1. General activity

Encourage the class to move around, through, over apparatus without touching it. This has the same purpose that a rider has when he leads his horse round the competition course so that he may 'sniff' the jumps. For the children this is the introduction to the size, spacing and layout of the apparatus. It also helps them to space well and keep away from other children and obstacles.

2. Warming up

Before the children are allowed on apparatus they should be thoroughly warm. It is dangerous for children to grip metal bars with cold hands. The body should be warmed up much as a driver warms up his car engine on a cold morning. So some vigorous exercises should be given, if necessary, to get the children warm. These activities could consist of jumps, rocking and such inverted exercises as can be achieved in the spaces between the apparatus. The actions may have to be limited to up and down movements because of restrictions in space.

3. Signals

It is helpful if the teacher establishes routine signals such as: 'when I say stop—slow down your movement, finish it and sit in a space on the floor'. This sort of instruction avoids children jumping or dropping off apparatus each time the teacher says 'stop' later in the lesson. It is not wise to speak to children while they are dangling all over apparatus or draped on bars or benches. It is important that children should realise that all the apparatus is for working on and any rest time should be taken by sitting on the floor away from the working pieces, including mats and benches.

4. First time on apparatus

Once discipline has been established and they are warmed up, the children should be allowed to use the apparatus. The most suitable instruction to give is, 'Move round the gymnasium, and when you meet a piece of apparatus get on to it, and find a way off.' This avoids a rush to leap over boxes and bars before the children have had time to test the height and texture of the materials. The emphasis is 'on' and 'off' and not 'over'. While children are moving about various suggestions could be made to keep the children alert and thinking:

'Have you been to every piece of apparatus?'
'Can you find another way off? Is there somewhere to climb down or slide down?'
'People on the ropes, come down one hand after another—do not slide down.'
'Remember the mats are there for people to jump on to—do not get in their way, walk round them.'
'Only jump off the apparatus where the mats have been placed.'
'See if you can find another way to get on to the apparatus.'
'Is there somewhere you can go upside down?'
Trampette: Children should never be allowed to use the trampette without very careful initial training (see p. 113).

As the children are freely working in this way, the teacher will be observing individuals and making assessments about abilities and needs. From what he sees he will begin to work to develop the skills the children need for their work to progress. For example, in the initial stages he will certainly have to concentrate on foot work, methods of recovery and inversion. The work the children learn on the floor they will gradually transfer to the apparatus. Some may use ideas they have learned in the same lesson, but others will take longer and need a greater familiarity with the work before they use it on the large apparatus. For example, a child may be able to balance on his head on the floor, but most children will experiment for a long time before they try to do this on apparatus.

5. Establishing routines for apparatus work

All the early lessons in the gymnasium will be devoted to forming good habits in the handling of apparatus and in gaining confidence in working on it. This will take up the majority of the time for at least a whole term. It is vitally important that sufficient time should be given to learning to get out equipment methodically and safely, especially apparatus such as frames and wall-bars that have to be pulled away from the walls and fixed to the ceiling and the floor. Routines for carrying benches and poles must be insisted on—so that each end is guarded by a child. All too often this aspect of the work is neglected and expensive apparatus, not to mention delicate bodies, are damaged by careless handling. Some schools of thought feel that this training should be emphasised before any serious work on themes begins and that theme based work serves to extend and clarify the children's initial free exploratory work. Others consider that work on simple themes should begin immediately, gradually introducing the apparatus a little at a time as is necessary to illustrate the theme. On the whole, frustration is avoided by letting the children 'have a go' and making the fullest possible use of all apparatus from the beginning. It is only when their movement becomes more skilful and sophisticated that children gain as much satisfaction from the exercise of their own bodily skill as they do from their use of apparatus.

While the work is still at the apparatus handling and exploratory stage there will be short warming up periods at the beginning of lessons during which the teacher can begin work on the development of simple skills. These will mainly be concerned with bodily skills such as recovery, balance and flight which will enable the children to work more safely on apparatus later in the lesson. The methods of breaking down these skills are found under themes. In the early lessons it is suggested that the following work should be covered:

Ways of going and stopping	p. 78
Ways of falling and rolling	p. 91-2
Simple balances	p. 44
Some emphasis on body shape	p. 116
Jumping	p. 89

6. Lesson plan for apparatus lesson. Before lesson—publish apparatus setting, put apparatus in right places in the gymnasium.

Activity	Organisation	Method of teaching
1. Running and stopping - with a) Change of direction b) Change of speed	Class moving freely about the space-concentration on keeping in a space of one's own	Direct instruction (i) Obedience to command (ii) Good spacing (iii) Silent footwork
2. Rocking from seat to shoulders	Individual spaces on the spot	Direct teaching
3. Rocking shoulders to seat to feet keeping ball shape	Individual spaces on the spot	Direct teaching
4. Add jump in air when weight on feet - then rock to shoulders	Individual spaces on the spot	Free practice - coach weight well forward over feet - high stretched jump - controlled fall back to shoulders
5. Jumps and landings	Individual spaces on the spot	Coach light landings
6. Running jumps	Watch spacing in travelling	Coach light landings
7. Running jumps one foot and two feet take off	Watch spacing in travelling	Coach take off from left foot, right foot, both feet. Work on landings
8. Take weight on hands	Individual spaces on the spot	Free practice. Coach (i) Correct hand placings (ii) Position of head (iii) Hips above shoulders (iv) Different leg positions

9. Get out apparatus	Divide into groups Place groups in apparatus position. Instruct each group in turn. Check each group's setting **Order of erection** (i) Fixed apparatus not ropes (ii) Large portable (iii) Benches and mats (iv) Ropes	Direct instruction. Coach correct methods of carrying – quiet placing of apparatus. Do not go for speed.
10. Free practice on apparatus	Individual spacing	Coach individuals, Emphasise landings, jumps, rocking, weight on hands.
11. Put away apparatus	Return to groups and put away (i) Ropes (ii) Boxes and portable (iii) Fixed apparatus	Direct instruction
12. Closing activity Practise weight on hands, slow motion.	Individual spaces	Coach very slow, silent movement.

A series of similar lessons will allow the teacher the opportunity for maximum direct control of the class in the early stages of their work in the gymnasium. Immediate establishment of good habits in the following situations is desirable before going to a freer method of working:

1. The starting and stopping of activity.
2. The habit of working in an individual space when still and when moving.
3. The habit of silent footwork and silent placing of apparatus.
4. Routine methods of carrying portable apparatus and setting up fixed apparatus.
5. Methods of forming and working in groups.

6. An efficient attitude to apparatus situations.
7. Short periods of free working.

When the teacher and class have arrived at mutual understanding and arrangements concerning the above points a more relaxed climate may be established and more difficult work undertaken.

USE OF APPARATUS IN CONNECTION WITH THEMES

Theoretically, with more advanced classes the apparatus setting should extend the range and difficulty of the movement ideas connected with the theme. The arrangement in itself should demand certain actions. For example, if the theme is *flight* the setting might provide gaps of various kinds, or may necessitate jumping from a swinging rope over an obstacle. So the apparatus itself suggests the task before the teacher clarifies it still further by making the task more specific. For example, the teacher may ask that each gap in a particular setting must be jumped by using a different kind of take-off.

1. Apparatus setting

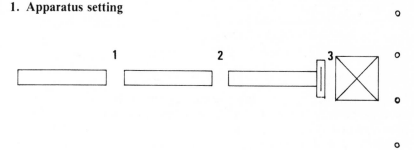

Fig. 7. *Apparatus layout.*

Three forms (Fig. 7):   one inclined wall bars, hip height
                           one flat
                           one steeply inclined on trestle, shoulder height
                           trampette and ropes as shown

Task   Gap (1)   Take off with left foot
                (2)   Take off with right foot
                (3)   Take off with either foot, land two feet on trampette and jump for ropes

Some teachers use task cards where the apparatus setting is illustrated and the task set. This saves time if used with a well trained class as the teacher does not have to keep the whole class waiting while she explains to each group what they must do.

Apart from extending the theme the teacher should ensure that the apparatus is set so that the specific objectives of the series of lessons can be achieved. The sequence tasks which are set should be closely related to the apparatus setting and designed at the same time. For example, on a theme in body shape one of the objectives could be to construct a sequence of movement which shows curled, stretched and twisted body shape. Such a task could be structured by the following apparatus setting.

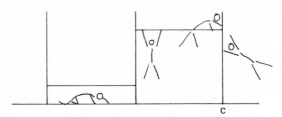

Fig. 8.

Poles and bars. Bars knee height and stretch height.
Task   Move *under* the low bar,
      along the high bar,
      from the high bar return
      to the floor using upright (c).

2. Transferring floor work to apparatus

Again in theory the exploratory ideas suggested in the floor work should then, in the same lesson, be applied to apparatus situations. Experience shows that many children cannot make the transition immediately. They are slow and careful in working out their ideas on the floor and then on the intermediate apparatus (see p. 36). Often they are not ready to immediately transfer the ideas on to the higher and more dangerous large apparatus situation. The teacher is then wise to retain in the present apparatus arrangement some settings relating to previous themes and tasks so that those who wish may continue to work on past ideas.

It is also wise to have at least one setting at which no task is given so that children may just 'have a go' and enjoy the freedom of simply doing what they feel like. In planning apparatus the following considerations are suggested:

1. The full exploration of the theme
2. The requirements of the objectives i.e. sequences
3. Settings from past lessons
4. Settings for free experiment

In one school it was decided as an experiment to strenuously work and coach the children on the floor work, choosing a particular theme and trying to achieve a high standard of performance connected with it. As a contrast in the apparatus part of the lesson the children were left to work freely, where and how they chose. The coaching on apparatus was confined only to improving the performance of what the child was trying to do.

The *themes* were weight-bearing, body-shape, and flight—in that order. It was noticeable how there was a time lag between success in the floor work and transfer of the same ideas to large apparatus. For example, during the lessons when the theme on *weight-bearing* was worked out on the floor the children merely explored the apparatus. When the theme on *body-shape* was taken, the children started to show some of the movements connected with the *weight-bearing* theme on the large apparatus. The following diagram shows the time-lag in transfer of movement ideas from floor to apparatus in this situation.

Floor work	Large apparatus
Weight bearing	Explore
Body shape	Weight bearing ideas
Flight	Weight bearing ideas including variety of body shape
Twist and turn	Body shape and flight

3. Coaching apparatus work

In practice it is unwise to push for results too soon. When the children are working on apparatus the teacher keeps various ideas in mind.

In the first instance his task is to ensure safety by the organisation of traffic of children and apparatus. Next he instils confidence by setting a calm climate of activity, unhurried and thoughtful. Always he watches the children carefully, observing and assessing their problems. Before setting tasks he will allow exploratory time. During the exploratory time he will coach the following points:

(i) Care in use of the body on apparatus

(ii) Clarification of action in the mind of the child

(iii) Extension of child's vocabulary of action

(i) It is here that the teacher demands control in the use of apparatus. This is stressed by the handling of apparatus; care in placing mats, stilling ropes after use, and lifting not dragging benches. It is also concerned with care of the body as it meets either the floor or apparatus, there should be no careless crashing and banging.

Actions should be repeated over again until they can be done with care or modified so that they come within the competence of the performer.

(ii) Even in free exploratory situations on apparatus movements should never be random or without thought. The teacher, in observing the children, will try to classify what any individual is attempting to do, so that he may be of help. If the activity seems quite random he can ask the child to repeat what he is doing. If the child cannot, then the teacher can continue with questions such as:

What are you trying to do?'
'What do you do on the bar?'
'How do you link one movement on the bar to the movement on the box?'
'What shape are you making in the air?'
'Is that part meant to be a balance?'

and continue to make him clarify in his own mind what he is doing, be able to repeat it, and finally perform it with care.

(iii) If necessary the teacher should be ready with suggestions of a general nature to extend the child's movement vocabulary. Work on apparatus always succeeds work on the floor, so ideas and practices on the floor can be recalled when children are on apparatus reminding them of the variety of activity already experienced. These general suggestions may refer to clarification of body shape, variation in direction or speed, different ways of take off, recovery, inversion or balance. Acquiring movement vocabulary is a cumulative process and children need continual reminding of past experiences so that they can use them again in different situations.

Vocabulary may also be extended by the use of frequent demonstrations so that pupils can see and appraise the work of their peers. Teachers should be warned to use demonstrations with care accompanying each with a commentary as to the values of each piece of work in relation to the person performing. Children should not be left to assume that they are meant to copy all that the teacher picks out for them to see—but should be led to see the principles behind the work so that they may apply them to their own specific problem. For example, a teacher should try to select several examples to illustrate a given point. (This point might be extension of feet to complete the line made by the leg. This could be illustrated by a leap in the air with extension of legs, a balance on hands, a roll, or a cartwheel. The teaching point is that whatever the action the feet are important to finish, extend and clarify the line of the body.)

For example, in extending the child's vocabulary of jumps many examples can be shown including jumps for height, jumps for length, jumps with a turn, with a variety of body shape, with a variety of take off and different recoveries. The child is led to a wider concept of the meaning of the word 'jump' rather than the imitation of certain specific jumps.

4. Coaching sequences

When the apparatus work has got beyond the exploratory stage and the teacher is setting tasks, his work is rather different. The teacher is now pushing for results. Although he is not demanding specific movements he is insisting on accuracy of response to the task. The actions chosen must be relevant to the task and the teacher should ensure this is so. He will therefore have to have very clear criteria in his own mind of what he will or will not accept and the reasons for them. The pupil is required to go further than clarifying his own actions, he must now conform to the task set by the teacher. The child is in a problem-solving situation. He will review all possible ways of answering the task and select the one that is best for him—according to his ability, experience and preferences. The teacher must help him in the selection of his movements, in the arrangement of them, in the technique of their performance and into a final pleasing form.

5. Selection of movements

Ways of extending movement vocabulary have already been discussed. How does the teacher help the pupil to select, what are the criteria? First must come consideration of the ability and technical competence of the performer. For example, the task might be as follows:

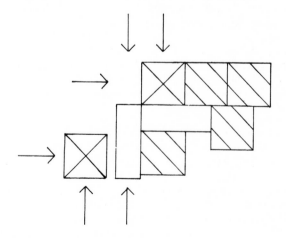

Fig. 9. Two trampettes, two boxes, four mats as shown.

Task Show a balance on hands, transfer to balance on another body part
and flight both on and off the boxes.

Balance on hands could be

a) on either box
b) on the floor

The second balance could be on the same box, on the other box, on a
mat.

Method of transfer is not specified
Flight could be on to or off floor

     ″   ″   ″ ″ ″ ″   ″ trampette from box or floor
     ″   ″   ″ ″ ″ ″   ″ box from floor or trampette
     ″   ″   ″ ″ ″ ″   ″ feet
     ″   ″   ″ ″ ″ ″   ″ hands or other part

Flight could happen any number of times

The sequence allows for change of level
                                         speed
                                         body shape
                                         direction

Secondly, in creating a sequence, contrast is needed so that once the first
movement is chosen it could flow into a contrasting one. The contrast
could be of body-shape, dynamics or action. Then the problems of flow
come in; the transitions between one action and another are very important
and also need to be varied throughout the sequence. Transitions occur via
stepping from one part to a non-adjacent part, rolling or falling or moving
through adjacent parts, twisting, jumping and tipping. The child is asked to
select the most suitable one for the situation. As the sequence begins to be
built up, more movements are added and these, as well as answering the
task, need to provide variety so that if the sequence has jumps and turns
and travelling in it, a movement to emphasise stillness or slowness may be
needed.

From such a list of possibilities the pupil makes the choices to form the
sequence which contains the specified actions. We have already listed the
following criteria of choice:

a)   ability   ⎫
b)   technique ⎬ of performer
c)   contrast
d)   transitions
e)   variety

There is, finally, the composition of the whole. The factors here are climaxes, accents, rhythm and pattern. The pupil determines which is the most important part of the sequence, emphasises this and then builds up to it and fades away from it. The whole sequence is a phrase; the climax could be at the beginning, the middle or the end, or there could be more than one climax involved. These main accents are the peak moments of the performance and can be emphasised by pausing, changing speed or sudden bursts of speed; they give the whole a pleasing and exciting form. The teacher by showing examples and by coaching tries to develop a sense of 'timing' in the pupil and awareness of rhythmic flow and emphasis.

The techniques involved in performance are developed and practised in the floorwork and are described under the various themes. The transitional or intermediate apparatus (benches and mats) continue and limit the floorwork and provide a useful link between the floorwork and the large apparatus. (See p. 35-7).

In summary the aims of the teacher when teaching apparatus work directly connected to a theme are to:

1. Clarify the set task
2. Suggest range of possible solutions
3. Assist individuals in their selection
4. Assist individuals in techniques of performance
5. Help determine the final form of sequence, with regard to its:
      shape and patterns
      rhythm and timing
      clarity of bodily performance
      technical difficulty and expertise

EXAMPLES OF THEMES

1 LOCOMOTION AND PAUSE

THEME: **Locomotion and Pause**   CLASSIFICATION: **Action**
                                    GROUP   **Introductory**

SELECTION

This is usually the first theme to be taken.

DEFINITION

This theme is concerned with the simplest and most basic ways of the body travelling and stopping. It is often used as the introduction to work in the gymnasium and is an exploration of the ways the body can move:

a) through the traffic of other moving bodies
b) over the floor
c) over, up, down, through and under apparatus

It also includes the ways in which the body may be brought gradually or instantaneously to stillness.

AIMS

1. To learn bodily control in the environment of the gymnasium.
2. To gain confidence in different ways of travelling and stopping.

OBJECTIVES

1. Form a sequence of the five basic jumps.
2. Travel by taking weight on different body parts.
3. **Mats and forms.** Travel along forms and across mats using different body parts.

4/5. **Large apparatus.** Choose three favourite pieces of apparatus and travel up or along it.
6. Show good starting and finishing positions.

MOVEMENT MATERIAL I   EXPLORATION OF THEME

A. Travelling on different parts of the body

(i) Travel on feet only using the five basic jumps
  a) one foot to the same foot
  b) one foot to the other foot
  c) one foot to two feet
  d) two feet to two feet
  e) two feet to one foot

(ii) Travel using hands and feet
  a) two hands to two feet
  b) two hands to one foot
  c) one hand to one foot
  d) one foot to two feet and other permutations, including crab-walking, bunny hop, catspring etc.

(iii) Travel on other body parts by
  a) bouncing on the same part
  b) sliding
  c) moving from one part to another; as in rocking and rolling.

B. Travel with changes of direction

(i) keeping high in air
(ii) keeping close to the ground
(iii) alternate (i) and (ii)
(iv) swerving
(v) sideways, forwards and backwards

C. Travel with changes of speed

(i) slowly
(ii) quickly
(iii) alternating (i) and (ii)
(iv) accelerating and decelerating

D. Ways of stopping

(i) sudden stop in small space
(ii) gradual deceleration to stop

(iii) from jumps
    a) **on balance**
        i.e. two feet together knees bent or one foot after other with knees bent and centre of gravity low.
    b) **off balance**
        i.e. with tipping into a rocking or rolling action.

MOVEMENT MATERIAL II   DEVELOPMENT OF THEME

A. No partner work

B. Intermediate apparatus

Mats and forms should be set round the gymnasium with each piece of apparatus equidistant from the next. The mats and forms should not be in close relation to each other.

All ideas in section on exploration should be tried out on mats and forms, each piece being used in a different way. Attention should be drawn to different directions of approach to the apparatus.

C. Large apparatus (see fig. 10).

1. Ropes.
    Task. a) Find ways up and down ropes (without sliding)
          b) Find ways of going from one rope to another.

2. Bars. 2 and 2a chest height, 1 and 1a knee height.
    Task. Move along bars using the spaces under, between and over.

3. Horizontal frame.
    Task. Move from one side to the other, without the feet touching the floor.

4. Two low boxes end on, mats as shown.
    Task. Move from one box to another and on to either mat without feet touching apparatus. Use different starting points.

5. Mats, ropes, benches.
    Task. Travel from forms to mats, and mats to forms by swinging on the ropes.

6. Bars. 1 at head height, 1a at waist height. Pole.
    Task. Find ways of travelling along, and up and down.

7. 3 benches.
        one reversed
        one on low trestle, one mat (short recovery space)

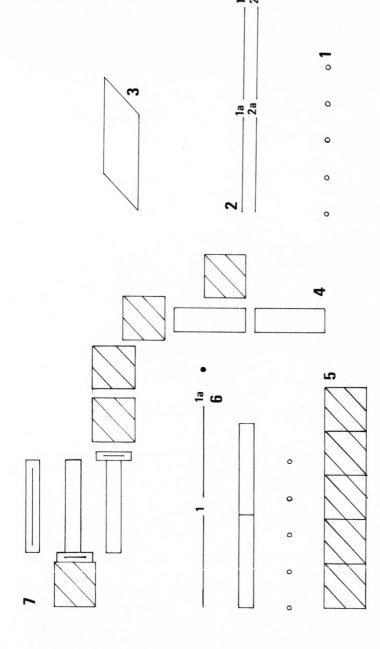

Fig. 10. Locomotion and pause apparatus layout.

    one on high trestle, two mats (long recovery space)
Task. Travel along benches (many ways)
    a) forwards
    b) sideways
    c) backwards
    and recover on mat.

2 WEIGHT-BEARING

THEME: **Weight-bearing**   CLASSIFICATION: **Action**
GROUP   **Introductory**

SELECTION

This theme is taken very early in the experience of a class. It could be the first or second to be worked. Most teachers begin working from a theme connected with travelling and stopping and then immediately move to this theme which is the fundamental one necessary to the understanding of gymnastics. From it stems all vocabulary of movement in a gymnastic sense, that is, the discovery of the full potential of the body as a moving instrument, and its ability to take weight on many different body parts.

DEFINITION

Weight-bearing is the experience of holding the body weight in stillness using a variety of different parts as bases. The body has broad surface areas which can support weight, such as the hips and the shoulders. There are parts of limbs which can bear weight such as the forearm or the shin—and there are small body parts, such as the hands and the head, the elbows and the knees.

AIMS

1. To develop control in holding the body weight over different body surfaces and parts.
2. To become more bodily aware by experiencing the security or insecurity, the ease or difficulty of supporting the body weight over its different areas and points.

OBJECTIVES

1. **An individual sequence** on the floor during the course of which weight must be taken on four different parts of the body in turn. One of these must cause an inverted position of the body.
2. **Mats and forms.** Using the forms for taking weight and the mats for recovery purposes—cross the forms three times using a different part of the body to support weight over the form each time.
3. **Partners.** Use partner to control body in weight-bearing situations where tipping or falling would otherwise occur. The partner will be used as a support or counterbalancing agent. Explore this idea both on the floor, the mats and the forms.
4.
5. Select three sequences or tasks from the large apparatus section.
6.

MOVEMENT MATERIAL I   EXPLORATION OF THEME

Weight may be taken on different bases:

Large body surfaces -	Back
	Hips
	Shoulders
	Tummy
Stable bases e.g. -	Head and two hands
	Two hands and one foot
	Two hands and shin
	one hand and two feet
	One forearm and one shin
Unstable bases e.g. -	One foot
	Two hands

(i)   Take weight on all the above parts. It is particularly important for beginners to practise various forms of inversion. The following stages of achieving inversion in two different ways are suggested:

Stages of taking weight on hands

1. Spread fingers out wide.
2. Bend knees and place hands on floor shoulder width apart.
3. Silently bounce feet up and down.
4. Look at imaginary cross in front of hands (to keep head from ducking between legs).
5. Repeat 3, trying to keep feet off the ground longer.

6. Repeat 3, trying to get hips over shoulders (Remember 4).
7. Repeat with twist in waist to return to different place on the floor.
8. Repeat 7, trying to tip weight onto one hand to cause a turn and twist together.
9. Repeat 3, swinging one leg high.
10. Repeat 4-8 with one or both legs straight.
11. Take weight in two hands—transfer to one.
12. Take weight on one hand—transfer to two.
13. Vary leg positions in the air.
14. Vary heights at which weight on hands is practised,
    e.g. form
        box top
        bar etc.

Stages of taking weight on head

1. Crouch position or kneeling.
2. Feel part of head where hair joins face and place this on floor or mat.
3. Place hands well back—i.e. towards feet thus making a stable triangular base.
4. Pushing with hands—slowly lift legs (which are bent).
5. Controlling weight with hands, straighten legs.

(ii) Take weight on a comfortable surface or a stable base and reduce its size, e.g. Take weight on two feet and one hand, lift one foot off the ground.

(iii) Practise holding the body in stillness, change weight to another part and hold still again. Make a continuous pattern of stillness and change to stillness, etc.

(iv) Add change of speed to (iii)—sometimes a slow change, sometimes a quick change.

(v) Emphasise the arms and legs as used in counterbalancing the rest of the body while it maintains equilibrium over different bases.

(vi) When weight is taken over a given body part explore possibilities of changing body shape, e.g. change from a stretched to a curled shape or a long thin shape to a twisted shape.

MOVEMENT MATERIAL II   DEVELOPMENT OF THEME

A. Partner work

(i) Partners copy each others movements, body shapes and sequences.

(ii) Partners assist each other in unusual or difficult weight-bearing situations, e.g. on hands, or one foot.

B. Intermediate apparatus (See layout page 36)

   (i)   Explore all weight-bearing situations (as in exploration section) on the different angles and surfaces provided.

  (ii) Begin to join movements together, i.e. linking two weight-bearing positions, while moving from one piece of apparatus to the other.

C. Large apparatus

The large apparatus diagram and tasks have been shown on pp. 38-40. They will not be repeated here.

3 TRANSFERENCE OF WEIGHT

THEME: **Transference of Weight**   CLASSIFICATION: **Action**
                                                 GROUP   **Introductory**

SELECTION

This is an early theme and should be taken after the introductory themes of locomotion and pause, and weight-bearing. In these two previous themes the children will have had many different experiences of transferring weight from one part of the body to another. This theme is taken next in order to bring to the conscious attention of the pupils what is already happening in their movement rather than to develop any new skills.

DEFINITION

This theme is concerned with the ways in which it is possible to change the body weight from one weight-bearing position to another. The focus is on the method of transference which may be stepping, jumping, tipping, twisting, sliding or rolling.

AIMS

To clarify the ways of transferring weight from one body part to another by classifying the ways and by:
(i) practising each method using different body parts.
(ii) selecting appropriate method for use in a variety of different apparatus situations.

OBJECTIVES

1. **Individual floor sequence** which includes transferring weight by jumping, twisting and tipping.

2. **Mats and forms.** A sequence using one mat and one form to show three different methods of transferring weight between hands and feet.
3. **Partner work.** No sequence, but be able to show how one partner can help another to transfer his weight from:
   (i) one place to another
   (ii) one body part to another
4. ⎫
5. ⎬ Select three large apparatus tasks.
6. ⎭

MOVEMENT MATERIAL I   EXPLORATION OF THEME

Weight may be transferred by:

A. Body actions of
   (i) **Stepping** - this implies taking the weight cleanly from one part to another, lifting the first part after the body is securely resting its weight on the second; stepping may take place between adjacent or non-adjacent body parts:
   a) from one foot to the other
   b) from one foot to two hands
   c) from two feet to one hand
   d) from one foot, to one hand, to the other hand to the other foot (cartwheel)
   e) from two hands to two feet (e.g. hand stand to crab)
   f) from knees to head and hands (head stand)
   g) from knees to seat to shoulders - pausing on each body part
   h) discover other possible body parts
   (ii) **Jumping** This action implies taking the weight clearly from one body part to another so that the first part is lifted from the floor *before* the second reaches the floor to take weight. i.e. there is a moment of flight during the transference. It may take place from one part to the same part or from one part to a non-adjacent part.
   a) five basic jumps: two feet to two feet
                         two feet to one foot
                         one foot to the same foot
                         one foot to the other foot
                         one foot to two feet
   b) feet to hands to feet
   c) other body parts to feet (off apparatus)
   (iii) **Twisting** Twisting takes place when one part of the body remains still and the rest turns, or when one part of the body turns one way

and the rest turns the other. Transference of weight by twisting
usually occurs between non-adjacent parts:

a) Take weight on feet, twist to place hands on floor, transfer
   weight to hands.
b) Take weight on shoulders, twist to take weight on knees.
c) Weight on head, twist to take weight on feet.
d) Weight on seat, twist to take weight on hands.
e) Weight on tummy, twist to take weight on back.
f) Continue exploration of weight transference by twisting from
   large area to large area, from small part to small part.

(iv) **Rocking** is the action of the body moving between adjacent parts
of the body. It may take place between:

a) knees and shoulders-   down one side of the body
                          down front surface of the body
b) feet and shoulders—   down back surface of the body
                          down one side of the body
c) with twisting—changing body surface of rock each time

Stages in transference of weight by rocking

Rocking—is the action of the body moving along adjacent parts of the
trunk and returning.
Method of introducing rocking:

1. Sitting—round back, grip knees and fall back on to shoulders.
2. Rocking action from seat to shoulders—continuous action.
3. On return from shoulders, speed up action, lean forward and take
   weight on to feet.
4. When weight is on feet, stretch hands forwards and stand up, return to
   rocking, standing every third or fourth time.
5. Repeat 4, instead of standing—jump into the air.
6. Lie flat on floor on tummy—arms stretched above head—lift arms and
   legs off floor.
7. Tilt body forwards by stretching and kicking legs—keep back arched
   and rock backwards and forwards.
8. Kneel up, move seat to one side and sit, return to kneeling.
9. Repeat to other side.
10. Repeat, kneel to side sitting to weight on shoulders—first on one side
    then the other. When weight is on shoulders, transfer weight across
    shoulders and continue to rock on the other side.
11. Continue rocking action, changing the surface of the body to be used
    by twisting the body when it is either on the shoulders or the hips.
12. Rock along back, balance weight on one shoulder, twist to recover

down front surface—continue rocking and reverse the action to rock
on back surface.

(v) **Rolling**
   a) backwards
   b) sideways—in contracted or extended position
   c) forwards
   Rolling should be practised and taught strictly in that order.

Stages in the transference of weight by rolling.
Rolling backwards.

1. Take weight on shoulders—stretch legs high in the air.
2. Touch the floor with toes of one foot and return to balance on
   shoulders—i.e. right foot touches floor on right side of head.
3. Repeat—but tip and let toes take weight and return to balance on
   shoulders.
4. Repeat 2 and 3 on other side.
5. Repeat 3—when weight is on toes, bend the knee and take weight on
   it—continue the flow of movement until the body weight is over the
   knee.
6. Kneel up.
7. Repeat 5 and 6 to the other side.
8. Speed up the movement.

Rolling sideways

1. Curl up body—tuck away elbows, bend head onto knees etc.
2. In this position, start with weight on knees (on mat) and tip over to roll
   across mat and return to knees.
3. Start on toes—still in curled up position and tip into sideways roll.
4. Repeat 3—tucking toes under so that it is possible to stand, or jump at
   completion of roll.
5. Repeat 1 and 4 on other side.

Rolling forwards (Teacher to help the first time)

1. Stand, just off mat.
2. Stand, feet wide apart, knees deeply bent—back very rounded.
3. Grip ankles with hands.
4. Tuck head between legs and fall onto shoulders
5. Repeat putting hands on mat close to feet and give small jump into roll.
6. Repeat starting one foot behind other.
N.B. Head never touches mat—shoulders are the first to land on mat.

(vi) **Tipping (falling)** From one weight bearing position, the centre of gravity is allowed to move outside the base thus causing the body to tip weight on to another part or a series of parts The hips often lead such movements,

e.g. falling from knees to shoulders
falling from feet to shoulders
falling from hands to forward roll
falling from hands to rock down one side of the body
falling from hands down front surface of body

Stages in the transference of weight by falling

Falling

1. Take weight on knees—tip hips slowly to one side, let weight of body gradually take over as body falls onto shoulders, rock back to kneeling.
2. Repeat 1 allowing the weight of the body to send the body on past the shoulders in to a roll.
3. Repeat other side.
4. Repeat from standing, the weight gradually passes through knees, hips, shoulders and over to knees or feet. OR it stops on shoulders and returns to feet.
5. Repeat from weight on hands.
6. Repeat from weight on head and hands.

B. Moving from one place to another

(i) Changing direction by transferring weight
e.g.
a) step into handstand - thus moving forwards: Tip weight onto one hand—thus moving sideways. Over-balance on to feet and roll sideways—thus continuing to move sideways then low and sideways.
b) Change direction of a roll with a body twist.

(ii) Changing level by transferring weight
a) To gain height—transfer from weight on feet on trampette to hands high on rope.
b) To lose height—weight on hands on box twist to land on mat with weight on feet.

(iii) With changes of speed
Explore the effect of a change in speed on the methods of weight transference suggested above.

MOVEMENT MATERIAL II   DEVELOPMENT OF THEME

A. Partner work.
Partner work is not relevant to this theme.

B. Intermediate apparatus. Setting as page 36.

Using the forms:
  (i) travel along broadside
  (ii) travel along narrow side
  (iii) travel along using floor and form alternately

Using the mats:
  (i) travel across
  (ii) travel diagonally across
  (iii) travel along one side

Using mats and forms in conjunction
  (i) move across the form onto the mat
  (ii) move from the form onto the mat
  (iii) move from the mat onto the form

Explore all the possible movement ideas listed in the section on exploration.

C. Large apparatus (fig. 11)

1. Two benches, one inclined trestle hip height, ropes, box, trampette, mats as shown.
   Task. Travel from piece to piece using only hands and feet.

2. Two boxes, same height, side by side. Mats and trampette as shown.
   Task. Move from piece to piece transferring weight from one body part to another as you go.

3. Bars 1 and 1a at hip height, 2 and 2a at shoulder height. Forms: one inclined on to 2a, one at angle under horse. Horse and mats as shown.
   Task. Move from piece to piece, the only restriction on choice of movement being that movement off the horse must lead into weight on hands.

4. Bars 1 and 2 about waist height. Wide planks, side by side, inclined onto bars to make a wide inclined surface.
   Task. Transfer weight up and down inclined surfaces from one adjacent part to another.

5. Three bars, 1 waist height, 2 head height, 3 stretch jump height. Mat under one end.
   Task. Twisting in and out of the spaces made by the bars, arriving on the mat with weight on a different part each time.

6. Springboard and mattress.
   Task. Jump over gap to land hands first. Gradually increase gap.

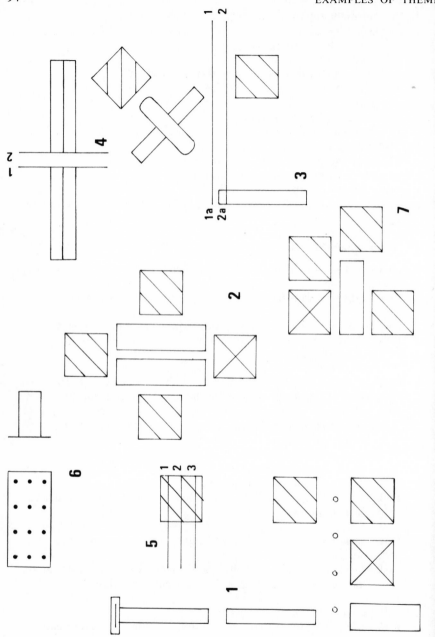

7. Box, trampette, mats as shown.

    Task. Land on box in balance on one body part, transfer weight to another part before leaving the box.

4 USE OF FEET AND LEGS

THEME: **Use of Feet and Legs**   CLASSIFICATION: **Body**
                                                    GROUP: **Introductory**

SELECTION

This theme may be used, or revived, at any time that the teacher feels the need to focus attention on the work of feet and legs. It could be used as the first theme ever taken with a class, or when the footwork of the class has become careless. Aspects of it can be used for one lesson at various stages of the work as and when the need arises.

DEFINITION

This theme explores the ways in which feet and legs are used in gymnastics for:

> travelling
> jumping
> recovery of body weight
> leverage
> swinging
> counterbalancing
> gesturing

It includes a study of the movements of the joints of the feet and legs and the use of foot and leg surfaces for weight-bearing.

AIMS

1. To concentrate the attention of the class on the importance of the work of feet and legs as the main means of body support and travelling.
2. To promote care and control in the use of feet and legs.

3. To strengthen feet and legs and to gain skill in their use.

OBJECTIVES

1. **An individual** floor sequence showing different ways of legs being as high in the air as possible and as near to the ground as possible.
2. **Mats and forms.** A sequence to show a series of leg gestures and shapes leading into and occurring in, flight and balance.
3. **Partners.** A sequence to include the following actions:
   (i) springing off partner using legs
   (ii) gripping partner with legs
   (iii) supporting leg(s) of partner
4. ⎫
5. ⎬ **Large apparatus.** Select three sequences from p. 100
6. ⎭

MOVEMENT MATERIAL I   EXPLORATION OF THEME

A. Actions using legs
   (i) Running, walking, galloping, skipping, hopping etc.
   (ii) Flight (see p. 108f)
   (iii) Landings—on balance
   (iv) Lifting and lowering body
   (v) Leg swinging—into jump
                          into turn
                          to initiate rocking action
   (vi) Transferring weight through legs to adjacent parts, e.g. rolling

B. Parts taking weight
   (i) Toes (one or two feet)
   (ii) Sole of foot (one or two feet)
   (iii) Shin
   (iv) Knee(s)
   (v) Hip(s)
   (vi) Side surface or back surface of legs (long or side setting)

C. Transferring weight from one part to another
   (i) **Parts of the foot**
      Weight can be transferred through the toes, along the sole (or outside edge of the foot) and into the heel.
      In stepping actions it can be transferred in the opposite direction, from the heel to the toes.

Practise of this action helps flexibility and strengthening of the muscles of the feet and ankles.

(ii) **Parts of the leg**

In raising and lowering the body, weight can be transferred through the foot, lower leg, knee, upper leg and on the seat.

In this movement and the return to standing using the reverse action, the arms and top of the body are used in an initiating and counterbalancing action.

D. Parts initiating action

(i) Toes may lead stepping, prancing, jumping

(ii) Heels may lead stepping, forwards, sideways

(iii) Knees may lead jumping, turning, wide stepping

(iv) Front surface of leg can lead swing into upward jump, side surface of leg can lead swing jumping sideways or across, or into turning and jumping

(v) Leg swing can lead body into handstand or inversion

E. Movements of joints of legs and feet

(i) Extension of ankle joint with flexion of toes is very important for the finish and line of a held position in flight or balance, or at any time when the feet are not supporting the body weight.

(ii) Flexion, eversion, inversion and rotations of ankle joint maintains flexibility of joint and strengthens leg muscles.

(iii) Flexion and extension of knee and ankle joint in raising and lowering the body. This action is very important for controlling the reception of body weight onto the floor, and the ejection of body weight into the air.

(iv) Flexion, extension, adduction and abduction and rotations of hip joint important in all stepping, levering and swinging of legs.

F. Legs to counterbalance

(i) With weight on hands. The position of the legs helps to control the balance on hands.

(ii) With weight on head or shoulders. It is easier, as with weight on hands, to balance securely if the legs are bent. The action is made more difficult by straightening first one, then both legs, and even more difficult by separating the legs.

(iii) Falling from balance in an inverted position. This may be both initiated and controlled by the action of the legs.

(iv) In bending forwards, sideways or backwards from standing, one leg may counterbalance the arms and trunk by moving in the opposite direction.

(v) In balancing on bars, particularly in actions such as in back somersault, the delaying action of the legs controls the movement round the bar.

G. Use of legs in body shape
Legs may be apart (wide or scissor shaped)
> together
> bent
> straight

when they are not taking weight. All possible variations using these shapes may be practised, both in stillness and in action. The practice of holding the still positions emphasises the feel of the body shape. In action, the student tries to recollect the shapes he has practised in an isolated situation so that the line of the body in the air will be clear.

MOVEMENT MATERIAL II   DEVELOPMENT OF THE THEME

A. Partner work
  (i) Find ways of take-off, using partner as apparatus
  (ii) Copy partner's individual floor sequence
  (iii) Assist partner's balance by supporting one leg
  (iv) Grip partner with legs
  (v) Lift partner with legs
  (vi) Throw partner using legs, or one leg and one arm
  (vii) Swing or turn partner using legs, or one leg and one arm

B. Intermediate apparatus (setting as page 36)
The forms may be used
  (i) for moving along
  (ii) for moving on and off while travelling along
  (iii) for moving over while travelling along
  (iv) for moving across and back
  (v) as an aid to take-off situation
  (vi) to balance on narrow side up and wide side up

Using the forms in all these ways and the mats for landing and recovery purposes, repeat the movement ideas suggested in the previous section on exploration.

In all this work emphasise care in the use of feet and legs for purposes of reception of weight and in the use of the legs in gesture and body shape.

C. Large apparatus
Any setting which includes ropes, bars, ejective apparatus, landing areas both high and low level, poles and frames may be used. Children may travel freely between groups and from one piece of apparatus to another.

General tasks may be set as follows:

(i) Find platforms from which to jump—land with resilience.

(ii) Find platforms to jump onto and hold still position on arrival. Use

    a) two feet take off

    b) one foot take off—both right foot and left foot in turn.

(iii) Find platforms where it is possible to land on other body parts, not feet.

(iv) Find places to grip with feet or legs.

(v) Find places to climb up.

(vi) Find places to hang up by

    the knees
    the hips
    the feet

(vii) Find places to grip with hands and feet, or hands and legs.

(viii) Find places to run fast and jump into the air, both uphill, down hill and along wide and narrow surfaces.

(ix) Balance on different pieces of apparatus showing

    legs wide
    legs narrow
    legs stretched
    legs bent
    legs separated
    legs together
    legs symmetric
    legs asymmetric

(x) Find places where leg swing is possible into turning actions or inversion using

    ropes
    poles
    platforms

(xi) Page 101 has been left blank for the reader to draw a suitable apparatus diagram.

5 CHANGES OF SPEED

THEME: Changes of Speed   CLASSIFICATION: **Dynamics**
                              GROUP: **Introductory**

SELECTION

This theme may be used at any time after a basic vocabulary of movement has been established. Themes on locomotion, weight-bearing and weight transference should be familiar to the students before attempting this theme.

It could be chosen so that greater control in the execution of movement is achieved, or in order to provide variety, accent and timing within the work already being done.

DEFINITION

All actions take up a certain amount of time. Gymnastic actions and sequences, once established, may be practised at great speed or very slowly. Acceleration and deceleration in travelling may be experienced and emphasis is laid on suddeness and sustainment in movement. Suddenness implies the maximum speed with which a movement can be achieved; sustainment implies a slow, controlled performance.

AIMS

1. To achieve greater mastery of movement by using changes of speed in the practice of actions and sequences.
2. To increase the student's awareness of the extremes of suddenness and sustainment possible within body action.
3. To gain experience of acceleration and deceleration in movement.
4. To increase the variety and aesthetic quality in the composition of sequences.

OBJECTIVES

1. **An individual** floor sequence containing:
   (i) One movement performed very slowly and evenly (with sustainment).
   (ii) One movement performed very suddenly, followed by a pause.
   (iii) One movement emphasising acceleration.
   (iv) One movement emphasising deceleration.
2. **Mats and forms.** A sequence on mats and forms in which all the movements are either sudden or sustained.
3. **Partners**
   A partner sequence to include:
   (i) a movement which brings partners together slowly
   (ii) a movement performed suddenly in unison
   (iii) a movement separating partners with deceleration
   (iv) any other movement emphasising a repeated accent
4.) **Large apparatus**
5.) Two sequences chosen from Section C on page 106.

MOVEMENT MATERIAL I   EXPLORATION OF THEME

A. Actions
   (i) Running, as fast as possible, with bursts of speed and sudden stops.
      No acceleration or deceleration.
   (ii) Walking—slowly, smoothly, evenly, silently.
   (iii) Accelerating, deceleration between (i) and (ii) forming a sequence, e.g.
      run fast using a straight pathway,
      change to walk slowly on curved pathway,
      change to fast run on curve and slow jog on straight pathway.
      Add stops in certain places.
   (iv) Using other methods of travelling (see pp 78) practise these:
      slowly
      suddenly
      with acceleration
      with deceleration
   (v) Contraction and extension of hands:
      slowly and suddenly
      with acceleration and deceleration
   (vi) Repeat (v) using the whole body.
   (vii) Repeat (vi) with weight on different parts of body.

(viii) Repeat (vii) using twisting and/or turning actions.
  (ix) Using any movement idea (i) - (viii) explore changes of level.
   (x) Using any movement idea (i) - (viii) explore changes of direction, with changes of speed. e.g. Change direction by transfer of weight from one body part to another, sometimes with suddenness and sometimes with sustainment.

MOVEMENT MATERIAL II   DEVELOPMENT OF THEME

A. Partner work.

Using the movement ideas in the last section, exploration, the partners should work in the following ways:
  (i) Matching movements
 (ii) Mirroring movements
(iii) Working towards each other
       around each other
       over each other
       away from each other without body contact
(iv) With touch
      grip
      or supporting each other
 (v) With change of speed in unison (both partners simultaneously) or in canon, (one partner following the other) or in opposition, (one fast while the other is slow)
(vi) With a pattern of sudden and sustained movements repeated several times with special attention being given to starting and finishing positions, and held positions during the sequence.
(vii) Repeat (i) - (vi) using mats and forms

B. Intermediate apparatus

Any arrangement of mats and forms similar to that on p. 36.
  (i) Link two movements together, one sudden and one sustained. One action should be on the mat and one on the form.
 (ii) Link three actions together, the first and last being sustained, joined by a sudden action.
(iii) Link three actions together, the first and last being sudden, with a sustained link.
(iv) Work on immediate changes of speed, with no acceleration and deceleration.
 (v) Work on a series of actions which are either accelerating or decelerating all the time.
(vi) Work with a partner, one partner changing speed to work at the opposite tempo to the other.

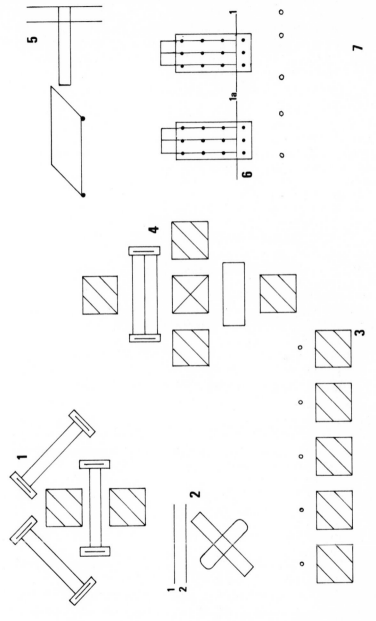

Fig. 12. Changes of speed apparatus layout.

C. Large apparatus (fig. 12)

1. Three benches on trestles, one at knee height, one at hip height and one at waist height. Mat as shown next to the bench at waist height.
   Task. Quick bouncy jumps on and off benches, moving from one to the other, using hands (if necessary) and feet. When on highest bench, spring high in the air and land. Go at high speed all the time.

2. Two bars, 1 stretch height, 2 waist height. Horse and mat as shown. Bench running under horse.
   Task. From a standing start move over, through, under, bars and horse keeping a slow, even movement.

3. Ropes and mats as shown.
   Task. Keeping hold of rope run with it, jumping and turning as the rope reaches the height of its swing each time—accelerating all the time, let go of rope and drop onto mats as rope reaches highest point of its swing.

4. Trampette, box, trestles waist high with planks. Mats as shown.
   Task. Quick jumps from one piece of apparatus to another, keep going, end on any mat.

5. Horizontal frame, two poles at corners. Two bars, form inclined on top bar.
   Task. Series of alternating sudden and slow movements, on and off the frame, round the poles; through, under, over bench and bars.

6. Ropes. Bars 1 and 1a at waist height. Two benches side by side, one coupled to each bar as shown. Benches covered with mattresses.
   Task. Accelerate using rope to arrive on benches which slope down and away. Decelerate using rolling actions down the slope.

7. Pupils select own apparatus and activity or keeping a setting from a previous theme.

6 FLIGHT

THEME: **Flight**   CLASSIFICATION: **Action**
                                            GROUP: **Intermediate**

SELECTION

When the class has experience of locomotion, stopping, weight-bearing and transference of weight, flight may be taken. This theme adds vitality and excitement to the work and leads to a variety of vaulting and jumping activities which are central to gymnastics.

DEFINITION

Flight refers to the passage of the body through the air while unsupported by the floor, partners or apparatus. The theme will include work on body-shape and action in the air, as well as methods of take-off and recovery. Assisted flight will be considered as part of this theme, the assistance being partial and afforded by partners or apparatus during some part of the action of flight.

AIMS

1. To experience flight through the air as high and as far as possible, and to acquire skill and confidence in this.
2. To explore all methods of take-off from the floor, partners or apparatus.
3. To practise the different forms of recovery that are necessary when arriving from a height, a distance, a turn, on or off balance.

OBJECTIVES

1. **An individual sequence** using the floor and including three different methods of recovery, one of which must involve inversion.

2. **A sequence in twos** (which may use mats and forms) showing at least three different ways of using partner as ejective apparatus.
3. **Mats and forms.** A sequence to show the variety of ways in which a form may be used to assist flight.
4. } **Large apparatus.** Two sequences on large apparatus conforming to the
5. } tasks set. (see pp. 113-5).
6. A sequence on large apparatus which involves the use of a partner.

MOVEMENT MATERIAL I   EXPLORATION OF THEME

The action of flight involves:
1. Method of take-off
2. Flight position
3. Method of recovery

A. (i)   **Method of take-off from different body parts:**
   a) Two feet - standing jump from two feet together, landing two feet together.
   b) Two feet - standing jump from two feet apart, landing two feet apart.
   c) Two feet - permutations of together/apart.
   d) Two feet standing jump - landing one foot.
   e) Repeat a) - d) taking a running start.
   f) One foot landing on the same foot
      the other foot
      two feet—together or apart
   g) Repeat f) taking a running start.
   h) One or two feet—landing on hands on floor or apparatus.
   i) One or two feet—landing on shoulders, head, seat, (on apparatus)
   j) From hands - to feet (or foot) (from partner, floor or apparatus).
   k) From hands and head - to feet (or foot) (from partner, floor or apparatus).
   l) From seat, knees, hips etc., (from apparatus).
   (ii)   **Parts of body initiating flight**
   a) Hands and arms help to gain height.
   b) Legs swing body into flight (particularly from apparatus).
   c) Legs can initiate flight from other body parts such as head, shoulders, seat - (from apparatus).
   (iii)   **Parts of body leading flight pathway**
   The flight pathway may be led by hands (as in a dive), head, as in a

jump for height or somersault, or feet (as in a long jump).
  (iv) **Spatial content**
      a) Flight can be directed upwards.
      b) Flight can be directed along, over gaps.
      c) Flight can be directed downwards (from height).
      d) Flight can take a curved, straight or turning pathway.
  (v) **Dynamics** - The emphasis here is on:
      a) The speed and tension for take-off
      b) The tension needed for holding flight position.
      c) The controlled release of tension for resilient landing.
      d) The increase of tension for sudden deflection of impetus where needed, as in a small or bent landing space.
      e) Tension needed to achieve the illusion of lightness.

B. The flight position and action
  (i) The flight position may involve a held body shape which may be:
      a) tucked or curled
      b) stretched, narrow or wide
      c) twisted
      d) symmetrical
      e) asymmetrical
  (ii) The body may take action while in the air such as:
      a) a turning action
      b) a twisting action
      c) a rolling action
      d) gestures of arms or legs
      e) inversion
  (iii) The pupil must experiment to discover the appropriate take-offs to achieve these positions or actions in the air, and similarly the appropriate recoveries from them.

C. Methods of recovery
  (i) Recovery on balance:
      a) on two feet, followed by knees bend and resilient recovery.
      b) on one foot followed by the other, with knees bent and low centre of gravity.
      c) on to hands, head or other body parts in balance (on apparatus).
  (ii) Off-balance:
      a) in large space—a running recovery or rolling recovery from the movement in the direction of body impetus.
      b) in small space with no room to run or roll, a quick deflection of body impetus UPWARDS onto another body part such as hands, side, shoulder etc.

(iii) From a height:
    a) onto feet as above.
    b) onto hands followed by roll.
(iv) From a spinning turn.
    Quick pattering of feet as body spins will prevent damage to knees and ankles.
(v) Over an obstacle—on various body parts, feet, shoulders, hands immediately following on with a roll to prevent jarring the body.

MOVEMENT MATERIAL II   DEVELOPMENT OF THEME

A. Partner work
(i) Using partner as an obstacle. Find ways of jumping over partner as he changes shape.
(ii) Sharing space with partner. On mats and forms keep up continuous flight on and off the form, over, under and round moving partner.
(iii) Using partner as ejective apparatus:
    a) Using partner's back with a one foot take-off
                          a two feet take-off
                      take-off with hands
    b) Using partner's arms, elbow grip for standing jump, running jump
    c) Using partner's shoulders, to push off (see pp 125)
    d) Using partner's hands as a stirrup
    e) Partner lies down, and uses a thrusting movement with his feet as mover jumps over him
    f) Partner lifts or swings partner and throws him into flight

B. Intermediate apparatus
Mats and benches are arranged in a similar pattern to the arrangement on page 36. In addition two trampettes should be added, one next to a rope and one near to a mattress. Spring boards and beating boards should also be set out with gaps between them and mattresses—as shown in Figure 13—1, 2 and 3.

All movement ideas suggested in the exploration section of this theme should be tried in relation to the intermediate apparatus—the most appropriate take off and recovery being selected by the pupils for each setting on which they work.

When they begin to work on a final sequence two people should arrange a setting suitable to their own requirements. They may then work on an individual sequence each or join together to compose a partner sequence.

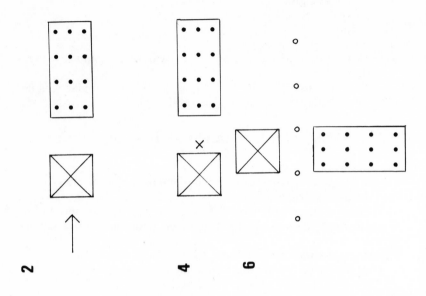

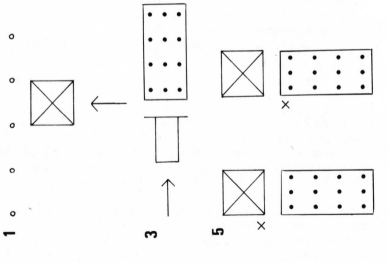

Fig. 13. Flight—apparatus layout.

Learning to use the trampette (Fig. 13—4)

1. Stand on trampette bed—two feet apart. Support stands in front of pupil holding both hands. Jump up and down, looking at trampette bed. Stop bounce by bending knees and cushioning the action of the bed. In jumping knees should be straight as feet land on the bed. The weight of the body on the bed causes the flight and springing action of the legs is not required. In fact it will deaden the effect of the bed.
2. Repeat 1 with support standing to side of trampette holding one hand (Fig. 13—5).
3. Repeat jumping action with support as 2. Jump on to mattress to recover.
   Support moves with pupil as he lands.
4. Repeat 3, support standing by but not gripping pupil.
5. Repeat 4 but pupil takes a short run, bounces once on the trampette to land on the mattress.
6. Repeat 3. Pupil jumps to catch rope then lands on mattress. (Fig. 13—6).
7. Repeat 6 with a run.
8. Repeat 7 with diagonal jump to another rope.
Each stage from 1 - 8 should be repeated many times.

C. Large apparatus (fig. 14)

1. Trampette, bench inclined on trestle, ropes and mats.
   Task. Trampette. Run, two foot take-off, leap for height up ropes, (grip one or two ropes, drop onto mats)
   Bench. Run up bench, take-off one foot to catch rope as high as possible. Land on a mat. Use each foot in turn to take-off.
2. Bench inclined onto very high trestle. Mats at end and sides as shown.
   Task. Run as fast as possible up inclined form, leap high, land on mat. Use each mat in turn. Landing must be on balance in a small space.
3. Low box (top and two lifts), mats as shown.
   Task. Run, land on box top, or over box top onto mats, with hands touching apparatus before any other body part.
4. Ropes, horse, bars, mats as shown. Bars, one knee height, one head height.
   Task. Run with rope swing onto or over horse or
   Run with rope swing through or onto bars.
5. Inclined bench from trestle (waist high), gap, second bench, mats at angles.
   Task. Run down bench, leap gap, along second bench take-off one foot to land sideways and roll. Use both sides of form, taking-off right

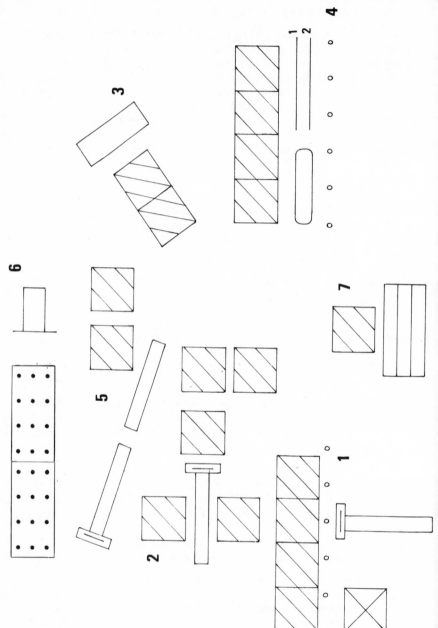

foot and rolling to the left, and taking-off the left foot and roll to the right. Do not turn and land with a forward roll.

6. Beating board, gap, long landing mattress.
   Task. Long run, one or two feet take-off to leap gap and roll on mats. Increase the gap each time.

7. Six forms making three steps. Mat as shown.
   Task. Run up steps, high jump making shape in air.

7 BODY SHAPE

THEME   **Body shape**   CLASSIFICATION **Body Action**
                                GROUP   **Intermediate**

SELECTION

When the class has a wide variety of movement vocabulary and control further refinement in the clarity of the work may be brought about by concentrating on the body shape. Within the action accuracy of body shape will be required. This theme should not be taken too early in the programme of work or static posing will occur; children will tend to emphasise body shape for its own sake instead of using it as a clarification of movement. Themes which should be covered first include locomotion, weight-bearing, transference of weight, flight. It is a good theme to follow that of 'flight' as it refers to the work on body position in the air and can be developed in other work following on from flight.

DEFINITION

In stillness and in action the body outline forms a shape. The theme on shape emphasises two main aspects: the shapes of the body when in a held position, as in balance or flight, and the changing shape of the body when in action. This theme is important in the development of awareness of the separate parts of the body in relation to the whole and knowledge of body position in varying situations.

AIMS

1. To give the class awareness of basic body shapes which include rounded shapes, long thin shapes, wide shapes in two and three dimensions, twisted shapes, symmetrical and asymmetrical shapes.

116

2. To experience and practise these shapes in held positions and in flight.
3. To experience change of shape in sequences of movement.
4. To raise the level of performance of movement from an aesthetic point of view. The look of the movement will become important.

OBJECTIVES

1. **Individual floor sequence.** This sequence must illustrate clearly in held positions the basic body shapes of curl, stretch, twist. One position must be in the air and one inverted.
2. **Mats and forms.** Create a sequence using mats and forms based on the same task as objective 1, but the movements into the held shape must be either sudden or sustained (see p. 102).
3. **Partner sequence.** Using either of the two sequences which result from objectives 1 and 2 learn partner's sequence. Be able to perform, therefore, two sequences in exact timing, body action and shape. The sequences should be performed side by side—i.e. shadow movements.

4.
5. } Choose three large apparatus tasks set in the Large apparatus section.
6. } They must be chosen from (i) - (v). Not (vi) or (vii).

MOVEMENT MATERIAL I   EXPLORATION OF THEME

A. Actions of contractions and extension and twist lead to held body shapes.
  (i) **Contract** the body round the central point e.g. umbilicus-curve the back and tuck away elbows, knees etc.
  (ii) Contract the body round other central points,
        e.g. the right side at waist level - bend right elbow towards side of right knee and stretch left side from fingers to toes.
  (iii) Repeat (ii) on the left side.
  (iv) Curl body round a centre in the middle of the back. This may best be done lying on the front of the body on the floor. Many young children can hold their feet or bring them over onto their head.
  (v) Experiment with contracting round other centres leading into semi-twisted movements.
  (vi) **Stretch** the body from tips of fingers to tips of toes in a long thin up-down movement.
  (vii) Stand on one foot and try to keep this long thin shape in a forward-back and side-to-side direction.
  (viii) Make stretched body shapes which move into three dimensions.

   (ix) Make a **twisted** body shape.

      All these shapes are made in static positions in an attempt to feel the shape kinaesthetically and learn to know where the various parts of the body are.

   (x) Join a series of contracting and stretching movements together.

   (xi) **Body shape in flight**

      Using various take-offs, achieve the body shapes already practised in tasks (i) - (ix) in the air.

B. Taking weight on different body parts

   (i) Repeating (i) - (viii) change the base on which the movement takes place,

      e.g. Weight on shoulders
                hips
                knees
                head
                hands
                separate parts such as hands and shin

   (ii) Explore the different parts of body which can lead into a particular shape:

      e.g.

      a) a wide stretch can be led by finger-tips and toes penetrating into space.

      b) a twisting movement may lead the body into a twisted shape. It may be initiated by the waist, one elbow, the head, etc.

C. Exploring space

   (i) The shapes may be taken to the limit of the body capacity or may be stopped part way—so that they are incomplete, but nevertheless show the shape clearly.

   (ii) They may reach upward into the high space, or sideways into the medium space round the body. There are many other diagonal high and low directions into which the limbs may go and which add variety to body shape.

D. Use of dynamics

The body can move suddenly into a held position and maintain the position with a good deal of body tension or the body can move slowly into the same held position. The former movement emphasises the end shape and the latter emphasises the pathway taken to arrive in this shape. In working on the sequences, especially the floor sequence, the practise of the movement both in controlled slow motion and in a series of sudden held positions will help the mover to give accent and rhythm to his work.

MOVEMENT MATERIAL II   DEVELOPMENT OF THEME

A. Partner work. Copying partner's sequence here has two functions:
- (i) It forces the performer to be very clear and simple in what he is doing and it is particularly necessary to emphasise the way in which the body shape changes,
  e.g. he must clarify which part moves first and how it moves and where it moves.
- (ii) It forces the observer to analyse what is being done and to imagine the movement and then perform it. Adjustment may have to be made to the movement pattern if one partner is more skilled than the other.

B. Intermediate apparatus
The sensation of body shape will now be brought into focus in the minds and bodies of the class. The mats give a comfortable surface on which to explore body shapes still further. The extra lift into flight afforded by the benches increases the possibilities of flight position and pathway. It is useful here to develop the concept of symmetry and asymmetry both in position and pathway. Symmetry in held position occurs when both halves of the body match in shape. This happens in a star jump, a handstand, most classical vaults, swallow dives and so on. In movement it occurs in walking, in a cartwheel, in a forward roll etc., where the stress on both halves of the body is equal. Asymmetry occurs where one side of the body is different in shape from the other and is stressed, such as happens when the body extends with a twisting action, or when one side of the body activates action in the air, or the body is suspended from apparatus by one arm or leg. If the asymmetrical movement is arrested and the body frozen it will be in an asymmetrical shape. An attempt to explore asymmetrical movement leads to flexibility, tipping, turning, twisting and off-balance situations.

Mats and forms (arrangement similar to that on p. 36)
- (i) Using different take-offs (see p. 109 flight) show symmetrical body positions in the air.
- (ii) Using a one foot take-off show asymmetric positions in air.
- (iii) Take a balance on form which shows symmetry in shape—change it to an asymmetrical shape by twisting or tipping before recovering on mat.
- (iv) Explore rolling over one shoulder or hip, so that weight is taken diagonally across the back during the roll. This movement may be initiated by one arm swinging forwards, across and downwards towards the opposite foot.

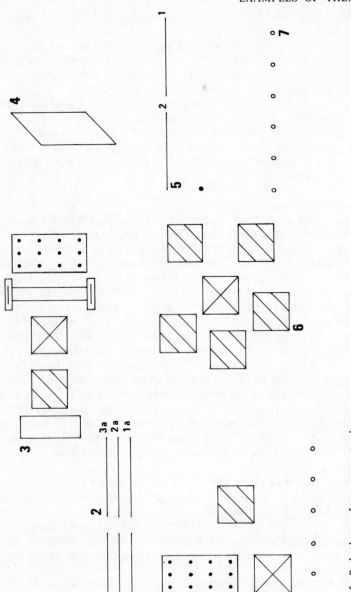

Fig. 15. Body shape—Large apparatus layout.

(v) In all situations discover the appropriate on balance or off balance recovery (see pp. 110-11) for the actions being tried.

(vi) Link several movements together showing symmetry and asymmetry consecutively.

C. Large apparatus (fig. 15)

1. Ropes, trampette, mattress, mat as shown.
   Task. Run, two-foot take off on trampette, turn in air to catch rope or land on mattress or land on mat.

2. Three bars, 1 and 2 very close to the floor and each other, 3 at stretch distance from bar 2. 1a, 2a and 3a to match.
   Task. Progress along bars by going between floor and 1, 1 and 2, 2 and 3 (possibly over 3) with bending and stretching movements.

3. Box and mat as shown, trampette, plank on trestles, mattress.
   Task. Jump onto box, land in asymmetrical balance, allow one side of body to lead into recovery onto mat, immediately spring into trampette into symmetric flight onto and off the trestle, landing on-balance on mattress.

4. Frame in upright position.
   Task. Partner sequence, matching movements, twisting all the time, using a rythmic timing to include a pause in each phrase. The pause to show a twisted shape.

5. Pole, bar 2 waist high, bar 1 jump to stretch height.
   Task. One hand on pole, find ways of turning round it, then round waist-high bar using asymmetric shape and high bar with symmetric shape.

6. Trampette, and mats as shown.
   Task. Show symmetric and asymmetric shapes in flight from trampette to each mat in turn.

7. Ropes.
   Task. Show symmetric and asymmetric shapes in inversion with ropes still and swinging.

8 PARTNER WORK

THEME: **Partner Work**   CLASSIFICATION: **Relationship**

                                            GROUP: **Intermediate/Advanced**

SELECTION

Aspects of this theme are used as soon as the pupils have some control in weight-bearing and weight transference. It is used as part of the normal development of all other themes. There are times, however, (an example is given on page 34) when it is taken for its own intrinsic value as a deliberate way of developing relationship between people.

DEFINITION

This theme encompasses an exploration of the relationships between two people engaged in gymnastic movement. The relationships are bodily, spatial and rhythmic. Body relationships are concerned with the interplay of body parts which may be near each other, touch, slide over, grip, lift or carry each other. The spatial and rhythmic relationships are concerned with different kinds of patterning in movement, floor patterns, sharing space, phrasing and canon etc. Working with a partner uses all previous movement vocabulary of both partners and extends and develops this by providing experiences which are not available to one person.

AIMS

1. To explore all possible ways of using a partner to achieve movements impossible to the individual on his own.
2. As a result of this to extend movement vocabulary.
3. To experience the adaptation and responsibility necessary when working with another person.

4. To recognise the talents and limitations of other people and to reach a better understanding of one's own.

OBJECTIVES

1. **Floor sequence.** Partners compose a sequence of matching movements to include flight, balance and inversion with changes of speed.
2. **Mats and forms.** A sequence using mats and forms to include:
   (i) Assisted flight
   (ii) Assisted balance
   (iii) Partners taking whole of each other's weight at some point
3. All large apparatus tasks to be completed.

MOVEMENT MATERIAL I EXPLORATION OF THEME
(Partners A and B)

A. Using partner as obstacle
   (i) The shape of the 'obstacle' can vary.
   (ii) The shape of the 'obstacle' varies as he changes the body part supporting his weight.
   (iii) As the 'obstacle' moves, the partner finds ways over, round, through it.
   (iv) A and B interchange in forming the 'obstacle'.

B. Copying partner's sequence
   (i) A makes sequence of actions, or
   (ii) Sequence of different weight-bearing positions, or
   (iii) Sequence of dynamic and spatial changes.
   B must
   (i) Observe
   (ii) Copy correctly
   (iii) Learn
   A may have to adjust his sequence to suit B's ability. A must teach B how to learn the correct body part involved, the correct spatial pattern and the correct timing.
   A and B should change roles.
   The sequence may be performed side by side (shadowing) or face to face (opposite sides of body used).

C. Sharing space with partner
   (i) Two partners sharing same space must avoid each other by going round going over and under each other.
   (ii) Two partners can chase each other round the same space, one

having to escape all the time and find varying routes over the apparatus.

The task demands that A and B do not move out of the prescribed area and must use the apparatus provided.

D. Rhythmic patterning

A and B select a rhythmic phrase and

 (i)   Keep the rhythm going as they move round the apparatus.
 (ii) A can follow the pathway and phrasing of B.
 (iii) A and B can share the phrase, each moving on one part of the phrase.

A sequence can be evolved using all these ideas.

E. Counterbalance partner's weight

A and B learn to assess each other's weight and then go on to assist balance on and off apparatus.

 (i) Experiment with ways of gripping (see p. 150):
     Shake hands grip
     Fireman's grip
     Elbow grip
 (ii) Keeping contact A and B turn each other
     In running and turning partner
     helping partner to jump
     rolling partner
     exploring other ways
 (iii) A and B face each other and hold hands, feet together and close—they slowly straighten arms and control the weight of each other.
 (iv) A and B stand facing, but apart. They fall forward so that their hands meet—their arms controlling each other's weight—they push each other back to standing.
 (v) A holding one of B's hands—controls his weight as he bends one knee and straightens it (the other leg is lifted).
 (vi) Repeat with B bending backwards to touch floor with hand.
 (vii) Repeat with B bending backwards to touch floor with head.
     (i) - (vii) The partner A must take responsibility for the other person and control the movement—both partners must find the best placing for feet.
     Partner B must keep body taut so that A can control it.
 (viii) Other parts of the body may be used for controlling another person's weight:
     A may be lowered and raised by B either
     a) using his back, or
     b) lying on his back and using his feet.

F. Taking weight of partner, Twisting, Lifting
   (i) A supporting - B keeping straight and firm so that he may be lifted.
   A lies on mat - B stands near, back towards A.
   A takes weight of B by placing feet against seat or lower back and controls it as B falls towards A.
   A pushes him back to standing.
   (ii) Repeat (i) with B facing A.
   (iii) Repeat (i), A lifts B away from the floor. A supports B's shoulders with his hands and his hips with feet. A returns B to standing.
   (iv) Explore other ways of controlling partner's weight by using hands and feet.
   (v) Repeat (iii) placing partner in a different place by lifting, turning and lowering him with hands and feet.

G. Throwing partner
Two principles have been used:
1. The supporter must be under the body weight of partner in order to lift him.
2. The 'body' must be firm and use enough body tension for the supporter to handle and control him.
These principles also apply to all lifting activities but in addition a mutual understanding of timing is necessary.

   (i) A makes *back* as for leapfrog, B pushes off with hands and vaults over B's back. This may be done with leapfrog action, or bunny jump or any other way of taking weight on hands.
   (ii) The movement (i) is repeated - at the moment B pushes off A's back, A gives a quick push up with his back to lift B. This requires exact timing.
   (iii) A makes a back on all fours - B uses it as a springboard. A gives a lift at appropriate moment.
   (iv) A stands feet wide, arms towards B, palms upwards. B runs towards A, jumps into the air, placing his hands on A's elbows. A grasps B's elbows, moves under him lifting him into the air and holding him there.
   (v) Repeat (iv) A throwing B in air.
   (vi) Repeat (iv) A throwing B at end of action.
   (vii) Repeat (iv) with B placing hands on A's shoulders and A supporting B under hips (see illus. p. 33).
   (viii) Partners find other ways of lifting and throwing each other.

A. Partners carry weight
   (vi), (vii), (viii) of last section lead into carrying situations. These may be developed further on large apparatus which assists the supporter by

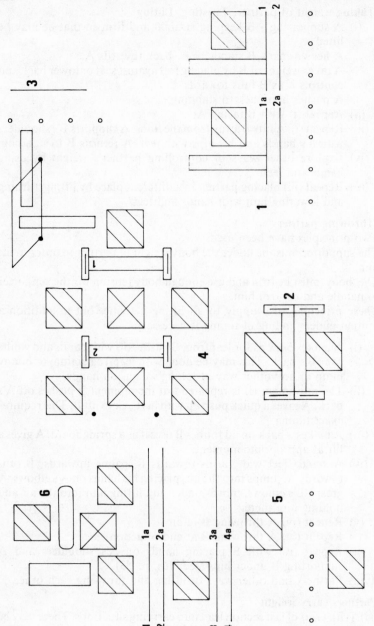

Fig. 16. Partner work—large apparatus layout.

already sending the body weight high from the ground. Ways of assisting off apparatus are suggested.

MOVEMENT MATERIAL II   DEVELOPMENT OF THEME

B. Intermediate apparatus

Examples of use of partner work and intermediate apparatus are given elsewhere, e.g.

> Action sequences
> Changes of speed
> Twisting and turning

It is suggested that the children themselves should arrange their own intermediate apparatus so that they may work on, and practise the aspects of partner work they wish. For the work on objective two of the theme, it is expected that they will arrange their own apparatus.

C. Large apparatus (fig. 16)

1. Ropes - bars 1 and 1a at waist height, bars 2 and 2a at head height. Forms inclined on bars 1 and 1a as shown, mats as shown.
   Task. Matching sequence in twos.

2. Two trestles high at one end, low at the other forming OXO shape. Two mats as shown.
   Task. Show assisted flight and balance on and off sloping surfaces.

3. Inclined frame, inclined forms as shown, poles at corner of frame, ropes, bar at chest height.
   Task. Make a sequence using a repetitive rhythmic phrase.

4. Trestles, 1 at waist height, 2 at head height, trampettes, mats and poles as shown.
   Task. The sequence should include:
       (i) Matching flight
      (ii) Partners going over and under each other
     (iii) Follow-my-leader sequence, at some time during the action.

5. Bars at height selected by students; mats, forms ropes as shown.
   Task. Carry partner at some point.

6. Horse, box, trampette, mats as shown.
   Task. Chasing over apparatus show moments of danger, e.g. near-miss situations, where one partner must take avoiding action.

N.B. The teacher, in his knowledge and wisdom, selects appropriate tasks according to the skill of his class. These are suggestions, not mandates.

9 TWISTING AND TURNING

THEME: **Twisting and Turning**   CLASSIFICATION: **Action**
                                   GROUP   **Intermediate**

SELECTION

This class should have a good basic vocabulary of movement, control in flight and balance, and an understanding of body shape. This theme extends the vocabulary even further. Themes which should have been covered include locomotion and pause, weight-bearing, weight transference, flight, body shape and possibly balance and overbalance.

DEFINITION

This theme emphasises the difference between twisting and turning actions by practise of these actions in isolated situations and within movement sequences. A turning action is a simultaneous movement of the whole body round a given axis and involves a change of front. A twist involves either the turn of part of the body while the rest is still or the turn of two parts of the body in opposite directions.

AIMS

1. To clarify the cognitive and psychomotor concepts of a turn and a twist.
2. To develop skill in the performance of these movements in a variety of situations.
3. To extend movement vocabulary.

OBJECTIVES

1. **An individual floor** sequence to include turning actions round two different axes and a twisted shape in flight.

128

2. **Mats and forms.** A sequence to include:
   (i) turning on the forms
   (ii) turning over the form
   (iii) balance on the form followed by a twist on to the mat
   This could be a matching partner sequence.
3. **Partner sequence** to include:
   (i) A turns B
   (ii) B turns A with a different action
   (iii) A and B twist apart from each other
   (iv) Any sudden matching twisted shape
4. ⎫
5. ⎭ Any two sequences chosen from Large apparatus.

MOVEMENT MATERIAL I   EXPLORATION OF THEME

A. The action of turning
The body can rotate round three axes:
   (i) **Vertical**—the axis runs from head to feet. Movements include:
      a) jumping with turning in the air.
      b) spinning on head, feet, seat, knees
      c) rolling sideways in extended/contracted position
      d) handstand, walk hands to turn on the spot
   (ii) **Sagittal**—axis runs from side to side through hip joints, waist or shoulders. Actions include:
      a) forward rolls on floor or round bars
         backward rolls
      b) standing - move to handstand, recover through 'crab' position
      c) handstand into forward roll
      d) handstand lower on to chest and rock
      e) rocking on back or front
   (iii) **Horizontal** - axis from front to back through waist or chest. Actions include:
      a) cartwheels
      b) travelling along a bar with a sideways swing
      c) any movement bending sideways
It will be seen that some actions listed involve a complete turn of the body through 360° to the starting point, while others only require a half or quarter turn to face a different direction.

B. Twisting actions
   (i) Either one part of the body is fixed and the rest turns
   (ii) Or one part of the body turns and the rest turns in the opposite direction.

   (iii) The body may hold a twisted shape in flight, or in balance

   (iv) Or it may use a twisting action to transfer weight.

     a) Stand—twist top half of body to right or left with a contracting or extending action.

     b) Jump—making a twisted shape in the air.

     c) Rock—twist so that change of direction is affected or a change of body surface.

     d) Transfer weight from one body part to another by twisting.

C. Combining twisting and turning actions

For example:

   (i) Prepare for a turning jump by twisting and contracting the body to one side.

   (ii) Run, swing one leg forward and upward and allow it to turn the body in the air, and follow this with a rolling recovery.

   (iii) Take weight on hands, twist legs to return feet to floor in a different place.

   (iv) Free practice linking turning and twisting actions with emphasis on transferring weight from one body part to another.

D. Turning, twisting with weight on different body parts

Taking weight on different body parts: e.g. head, shoulders, knees, hips etc. and one hand, one knee, etc. (see p. 85f)

   (i) Turn

     a) Pivot on weight-bearing part

     b) Roll away from weight-bearing part

     c) Turn round axis with transference of weight

       e.g. Transfer weight from feet to hands to feet turning round sagittal axis

   (ii) Twist

     a) Take weight on different parts and make static twisted shape

     b) Twist and take weight on another part—by tipping or stepping (placing)

Examples

with weight on hands, twist to take weight on feet;

with weight on head twist to take weight on knees;

with weight on knees twist to take weight on shoulders;

with weight on shoulders tip off balance and take weight through back and twist on to knees etc.

E. Different parts of body leading the action

   (i) Turns, e.g.

     a) Arms may swing the body into a spin

     b) Arms may turn the body in the air

c) A leg can turn the body in a spin or in the air
d) Elbow can lead the body into cartwheel
e) Hand can lead the body into turn round a bar
f) Knees can lead the body into a roll, from lying etc.

(ii) Twists

Parts of the body can lead the body into a twisting pathway, e.g.

a) Standing—hands lead the body twist to right or left before springing to take weight on them
b) Weight on shoulders, feet can lead body over the head and into change of weight over one shoulder onto front of body
c) Knees can lead twist out of handstand
d) Standing, hips can lead twist into roll

F. Time, force, space

(i) Space

a) Explore twisting and turning movements that lead the body high into the air, or close to the ground
b) Explore twisting and turning movements which cause a change of direction in pathway of movement
c) Link twisting and turning movements using changes of level and direction

(ii) Dynamics

a) Perform all actions in slow motion
b) Perform all actions suddenly
c) Link actions together and stress a change of speed, as well as direction and level

MOVEMENT MATERIAL II   DEVELOPMENT OF THEME

A. Partner work

(i) A makes shape;
B turns and twists under and over, round and through partner's body.

(ii) Copy partner's floor sequence (Objective 1) and be able to perform it simultaneously.

(iii) Grip hands, stand side to side or facing: find ways of turning and spinning partner. Use rolls, supported jumps, spine—while maintaining contact.

(iv) Use partner as spring board for turning jumps, vaults or somersaults,
e.g. his back
his hands
his shoulders

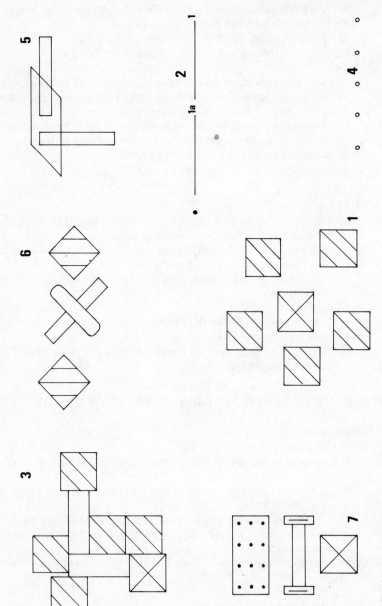

Fig. 17. Twist and turn—Large apparatus layout.

B. Intermediate apparatus (setting see p. 36)

  (i) **Mats** Turning movements.

  (ii) **Benches**

    a) Turning movements on the bench

    b) Turning movements over the bench

    c) Twisted position in balance on bench

    d) Twisted action from balance on bench into recovery on mat

    e) Twisted shape in flight from bench

    f) Twisted shape in flight over the bench

    g) Varying take-offs—one foot or two—and leading into twisting and turning in air

  (iii) **Mats and benches**

    Link twisting and turning movements which change direction, level, speed and confine themselves to the space indicated by mats and forms.

  (iv) Compose sequence (Objective 2)

C. Large apparatus (fig. 17)

1. Trampette - with bed in flat position. Surrounded by mats.

  Task. a) Two-foot take-off on trampette, turn in air, land on any mat.

      b) Two-foot take-off on trampette, show twisted position in air, land on any mat.

2. Bars - 1 at jump stretch height - 1a at waist height - pole.

  Task. a) Swing side to side or front to back on bar in stretch position.

      b) Travel along using hands.

      c) Find other ways of turning round bar.

      d) Find ways of spinning or turning round pole—link chosen movements to form sequence.

3. Trampette, two boxes, mats as shown.

  Task. Make a sequence to include:

      a) Turning movement on the box.

      b) A turning movement off the box on to the mat.

      c) One transition involving a twist.

4. Ropes.

  Task. Explore possibilities of turning using ropes and floor. Select three ways and form sequence.

5. Angled frame, two benches inclined on to it.

  Task. Travel from one surface to the next, diagonally. Form a short matching sequence in twos.

6. Horse - bench running under. Mats as shown.

  No task. Free practice.

7. High trestles, bench slung between, mattress, trampette.
   Task. Run, take off on trampette with two feet, hold twisted body
   shape on or over the bench, recover on mattress.

10 RISING AND FALLING

THEME: **Rising and Falling**   CLASSIFICATION: **Action**
                                   GROUP: **Intermediate**

SELECTION

Many children find difficulty in making transitions from one spatial level to another with control and fluency. This theme should be used with classes where pupils cannot lower the whole or parts of their bodies with control, or who find difficulty in lifting their bodies from a low level without a break in movement. This theme should precede work on levels.

DEFINITION

The body or parts of the body may be raised through flight, swinging, stretching, climbing, or balancing over a fixed point: falling may be controlled by counterbalance, elastic landing, and transference of weight on to adjacent body parts.

AIMS

1. To develop strong use of the body in elevation through springing, swinging, stretching and balance.
2. To enable children to move into high space levels with fluency.
3. To encourage confidence and care in lowering the body or parts of the body with control.

OBJECTIVES

1. An individual floor sequence showing different ways of achieving elevation and control in lowering the body.

2. Mats and forms. A sequence to show springing and balancing at different levels, using counterbalance and rolling to control the body when falling.
3. Partners. A sequence to show each person helping a partner achieve elevation and lowering a partner with control.

4
5 } Large apparatus. Select three tasks from p. 139
6

MOVEMENT MATERIAL I   EXPLORATION OF THEME

A. Elevation
  (i) **Springing**
    a) Using both feet to take off, practise springing from standing and with a run.
    b) Taking off from one foot, practise springing on one foot (hopping).
    c) Take off from one foot and land on the other, with and without run-up.
    d) Vary springing action to elevate other parts of the body, e.g. hips, back, leg.
  (ii) **Swinging**
    a) Using free body parts to swing the body into flight (see p. 154f).
    b) Start in crouched or kneeling position: swing arms to bring head high.
    c) From low spatial position, swing leg to take body weight higher in inversion, e.g. headstand, handstand.
  (iii) **Stretching and balancing**
    a) Stretch parts of the body suddenly and strongly to bring the body higher.
    b) Stretch the whole body slowly over its base to reach a higher level.

B. Lowering
  (i) **Counterbalance**
    a) From a balance on one knee, take the weight on to the hands in front, counterbalancing with one leg behind (on mats). Develop this task until falling on to the hands can be achieved with control from a standing position.
    b) Use different weight-bearing parts and transfer the weight on to free body parts with varying body parts being used for counterbalance.

    c) Develop the task so that falling can be controlled forwards, backwards and sideways.

 (ii) **Landings**

    a) Practise elastic landing from a height on to 2 feet and 1 foot.

    b) Practise landing from a running leap by 'running out' of the jump.

    c) Taking weight on hands, allow joints of hands, arms and shoulders to 'give' as weight is received, before transferring weight to other body parts: progressively increase speed to improve arm strength.

(iii) **Transference of weight** (on mats)

    a) From seat, tip off balance and take weight on side, front or back on successive body parts to control fall by rolling or rocking.

    b) From knees, take weight on thighs, hips, back, and shoulders in the same way.

    c) Varying bases, practise increasingly quick weight transference on adjacent body parts.

    d) Practise lowering the body by controlled use of joints, e.g. over two feet, 1 foot, two hands (with support), one hand and one knee.

C. Changing levels

Use the skills practised to move fluently from one level to another: possibly at first only one level change may be achieved. Later, as the body learns to think ahead, several rises and falls can be achieved in one sequence of movement.

MOVEMENT MATERIAL II   DEVELOPMENT OF THEME

A. Partner work

   (i) Use of legs and back in lifting and lowering partner's weight.

  (ii) Act as counterbalance to partner in lowering.

 (iii) Help partner to get body high, e.g. assisted springing, swinging.

 (iv) Use of different grips between partners in receiving weight.

B. Large Apparatus

  1. Double bars, hip height and 'easy reach' height, one form inclined to the floor from bottom bar, towards box; one form on floor parallel to box under inclined form.

  2. Frame, with parallel from under trestle top, mat.

  3. Box, form, upturned form, horse without pommels and springboard, mat.

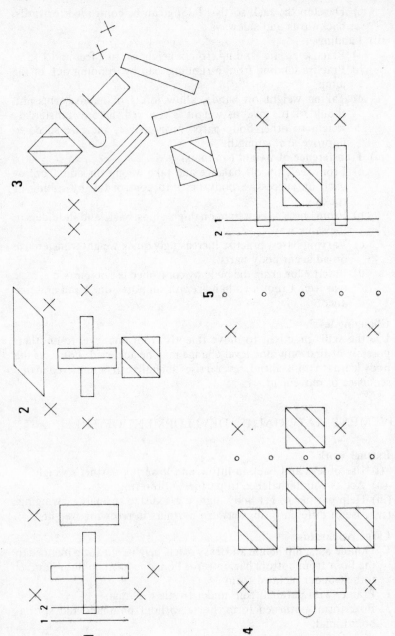

Fig. 18. Rising and falling—large apparatus layout:

4. Trampette, ropes, mat, springboard, horse end on with form on floor under horse, mats.
5. Ropes, double bars, waist height and swing height; two forms inclined from bottom bar, mat.

Tasks: to be used where appropriate on apparatus
  (i) Climb vertical pieces of apparatus, trying to achieve rhythm in gripping and releasing.
 (ii) Find ways of getting from horizontal pieces of apparatus to others of different levels.
(iii) Practise landing from high apparatus on mats and on other pieces of apparatus.
 (iv) Use ropes to swing the body on to or over a high piece of apparatus.
  (v) Use the arms to lower the body from the apparatus on to the floor.
 (vi) Try to get different parts of the body high and vary the body parts receiving the weight when coming off apparatus.

11 LEVELS AND DIRECTIONS

THEME: **Levels and Directions**   CLASSIFICATION: **Space**
                                        GROUP: **Various**

SELECTION

This theme presupposes some vocabulary of movement. Aspects of this theme are apparent in every lesson taken in educational gymnastics. In the early lessons the awareness of space, when many people are working in a crowded room, is very important. In advanced work, when students are selecting and setting their own apparatus, the relationship of one piece to another is largely determined by the need for change of level and direction in pathway, the provision of high and low gaps and surfaces. The theme would probably be taken in its entirety with a class of very skilled traditional gymnasts whose movement has been habitually limited spatially.

DEFINITION

The purpose of this theme is to emphasise the relationships of movement to its spatial contexts. These are:
   (i) the directions of the pathway taken by the moving body in relation to the floor, apparatus and other people;
   (ii) the directions, pathway and shape of the movement itself;
   (iii) the direction and pathway of the body, or parts of the body of the moving person.

AIMS

1. To extend the understanding of movement principles by focusing the attention of children on the spatial aspects and possibilities of bodily action.

These include:
   (i) the area round the body in which it is possible for various parts to
        move.
  (ii) the space in a given room where it is possible for the body, and parts
        of the body to move. This will include the space near the ground
        and the space into which it is possible to jump, with and without the
        help of apparatus.
2. To explore all possible pathways of movement along the ground, over
   apparatus and into the air. This will include straight, curved and twisted
   pathways in the vertical, horizontal and frontal planes.
3. To extend movement vocabulary as new areas of space are explored by
   different parts of the body.

OBJECTIVES

1. **Individual floor sequence** to show a variety of movements in which
   hands move as high in the air as possible then onto the ground, then feet
   move as high in the air as possible then onto the ground.
2. **Mats and forms.** Show a sequence on the mats and forms in which the
   movements include actions in forward, backward, sideways and diagonal directions. The directions to be in relation to the body of the
   mover and not the apparatus or the room.
3. **Partner sequence on mats and forms** in which partners, moving in
   relation to each other show pathways—both on the floor and in the air
   which are straight, curved or twisted.
4. **Large apparatus.** One sequence where pathway goes from
   High—low—high—low.
5. One sequence where pathway shows constant changes of direction.
6. One sequence involving circular movement of body or pathway.

MOVEMENT MATERIAL I   EXPLORATION OF THEME

A. Levels
   (i) **The body in space**
       The body moves high in flight
           with turns, twists, extension
       The body moves low with falls, rolls and all ways of
           travelling close to the ground
   N.B. In advanced work the body can roll high - as in a flying somersault.
   (ii) **Parts of the body in relation to each other.**
        Parts of the body can move high in relation to the rest.

The chest can be high in a jump
The head can be high in a balance
    knees can be high when weight is on shoulders
    hips can be high when weight is on hands
    tummy can be high in crab position

Hands and head go low in dive roll—hips go low in a fall. It is both the fact of the body being high or low *and* the sensation of 'highness' or 'lowness' that we are concerned with here. The sensation of 'highness' refers to the lift of the body away from the ground and the focusing of attention upward and is desirable in all flight and many balanced positions.

B. Pathways

(i) Actions in space

Pathways may be straight, curved or twisted.

e.g.

a) Running with swerves	Pathway is curved
b) Running with change of direction	Pathway is zig zag
c) A spinning jump	Pathway is circular
d) Swinging on a rope	Pathway is curved
e) Turning round a bar	Pathway is circular
f) Twisting in and out of frame	Pathway is twisted
g) Jumping to catch bar	Pathway is straight
h) Jumping to catch bar and turning	Pathway is straight then curved

(ii) The body in movement - including changing body shape (see p. 117-8)

The body assumes the shape in movement most likely to encourage the action, e.g.

a) Curved shape	rolling
b) Pin shape	diving to catch bar or rope
c) Spread wide	to lift a person
d) Long narrow	to swing or rotate round bar
e) Wide	to balance

C. (i) Direction in relation to the room, the setting of apparatus.

Look at large apparatus setting to see how the body direction and level is *determined by* the apparatus which demands

    Up and down (high and low) movement
    Zig zag movement
    Circular movement
    Twisted movement
    Rolled up movement
    Curving movement

(ii) Movement in relation to the person

Movements may be forwards, backwards, sideways or diagonal to the body of the mover, e.g.

Forwards	run, jump over a gap
	forward roll
	hand stand
Sideways	cartwheel, gallop steps
	falling from knees to shoulders
	falling from hands down one side of the body
Backwards	standing move to crab position
	backward roll
	back somersault

In spatial terms a forward roll

is forward in relation to mover
curved in pattern of movement and body
shape straight in floor pattern
low in the room

MOVEMENT MATERIAL II   DEVELOPMENT OF THEME

A. Partner work

(i) Help partner to move high into the air.

(ii) Match partner's directional sequence.

e.g.

Stand, side by side - one yard apart
forward roll - stop movement with weight on shoulders.
fall from shoulders to knees
back roll to stand and
jump in air followed by immediate
cartwheel and side roll.

Order of movements here forward, sideways, backwards, high, sideways and sideways low.

B. Mats and forms

In conjunction with partner - explore pathways which go over, round and through each other and apparatus.

C. Large apparatus (fig. 19)

1. High bars 2 and 3 - form slung between. Two trampettes, pole, mats and ropes.

Task. Move high-low-high-low-high continuously between trampettes, bars, bench, poles, ropes etc.

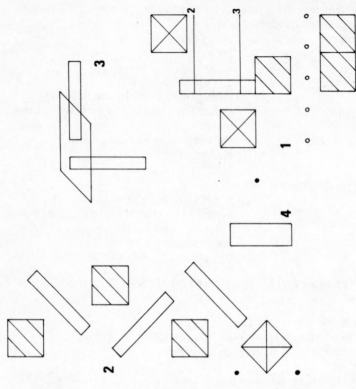

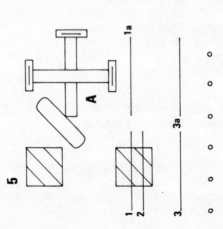

Fig. 19 Levels and directions—large apparatus layout.

2. Forms, mats, trampette, poles to form zig zag pattern as shown.
   Task. Make zig zag pathway using forms, trampette, pole or curved pathway using mats and pole.

3. Frame - Vertical position. Benches inclined at different sides and levels.
   Task. Show twisted pathway using floor, frame and benches.

4. Box (not too high)
   Task. Approach from different directions - change direction on box and leaving in another direction - keep up continuous action on the box by members of the group.

5. Horse, angled, two legs high, two low; inclined form on trestle going up to horse, form on high trestles crossing sloping form; mats as shown. Bars 1a chest height, 1 stretch height, 2 knee height.
   Task. Explore angled pathways and varying heights and levels forming a continuous sequence of movement beginning and ending at A.

6. Bars, 3 chest height, 3a waist height and ropes.
   Task. Make continuous circular movements using bars, floor and ropes.

12 USE OF HANDS AND ARMS

THEME: **Use of Hands and Arms** CLASSIFICATION: **Body**
                                                 GROUP: **Intermediate**

SELECTION

This theme can appear anywhere in the hierarchy, and aspects of it may need constant repetition especially for girls and women. It focuses attention on the importance of accurate and efficient use of hands and arms and the aesthetic value of hand and arm positions.

DEFINITION

This theme emphasises the use of hands and arms in many ways and particularly in their weight-bearing capacity. The body weight can be supported over or under the hands and arms or even parallel to them in horizontal and vertical situations. The hands and arms can receive weight from flight situations on the floor, and on still and moving apparatus. The movements of the joints of the hands and arms in gripping, rotation, flexion and extension can be explored, and their use in counter-balance, initiation of movement, in gesture and in body shape can be experienced. The role of hands and arms in the control of a partner's weight is included.

AIMS

1. To strengthen hands and arms and gain skill and confidence in their weight-bearing function.
2. To emphasise the importance of hands and arms as controlling factors in gymnastic situations.
3. To focus attention on the correct and varied use of hands and arms in gesture and every day movement.

147

OBJECTIVES

1. **Individual floor sequence** to include movements where:
   (i) the weight is taken on both hands
   (ii) the weight is transferred through hands to some other part
   (iii) the arms initiate a turning action
2. **Partner sequence** to show three ways in which hands and arms may assist the action of a partner.
3. **Mats and forms** A sequence which includes taking the weight of the body over the hands:
   (i) on the form
   (ii) one hand on form, one on floor
   (iii) on the mat

4.⎫
5.⎭ Select two **large apparatus** sequences:

   (i) where the weight is supported over the hands
   (ii) where the weight is taken under the hands

MOVEMENT MATERIAL I   EXPLORATION OF THEME

   (i) Hands and arms may **support the body weight**:
       a) with arms straight ⎫ in both cases the body weight
       b) with arms bent   ⎬ may be over or under the hands.
       c) with one arm straight and one bent, on a stepped surface or in a half-hang, half-vault situation between two bars.
   (ii) Hands and arms may **assist other parts to take weight**:
       a) hands assist head.
       b) hands and one foot etc.
       c) forearm and shin etc.
       d) arms and one shoulder.
       e) hands and one shoulder
   (iii) **Transferring weight** through arms:
       a) Landing on arms and transferring weight into forward roll. Arms reach out and are used as a braking factor.
       b) Movements may pass from hand to hand as in a cartwheel or from two hands to one—as in arab-spring—or one to two as in walking on hands.
       c) From balance on hands, one or both arms may be slowly bent to effect a forwards roll or a rock down one side of the body.
   (iv) Arms may be **used as levers**:
       a) to lift the body—as in jumps of all kinds—the upswing of the arms lifts the body or the forward swing helps it to clear a long, horizontal gap.

    b) the arms can turn or twist the body in the air. The sudden action of the arms can turn, twist, or spin the body in the air after take-off—both in jumping and in diving and on the trampoline.

(v) Arms may be used as **counterbalancing agents:**
    a) In balances on one foot; forward, backwards or sideways.
    b) In bending backward, the position of hands and arms—in front of or behind the body helps to control the lowering of the body.
    c) In taking large steps in any direction the arms lengthen the counter-balancing effect of the trunk as it moves in the opposite direction.
    d) In balances on one knee, or hips.

(iv) Arms are important in **body shape**—to create symmetry, or asymmetry in flight and in balance. In body shape the hands may be together or apart—near to feet or far from them. The relationships between hands and feet in gymnastic actions are manifold, for example:
    a) as far apart as possible in a cartwheel.
    b) hands close together, feet close together, but feet far from hands in a hand stand.
    c) hands and feet as close together as possible in a roll or a pike jump.
    d) right hand and foot together, left hand and foot together—but feet wide apart in a pike stride jump.

MOVEMENT MATERIAL II   DEVELOPMENT OF THEME

A. Partner work
Hands and arms are important in the following aspects of partner work:
  (i) Assisted balance
  (ii) Assisted flight
  (iii) Swinging and turning partner
  (iv) Lifting and carrying and throwing partner
  (v) Supporting partner in recovery situations
The following aspects must be explored:.
  (i) Gripping with hands
  (ii) Gripping with arms
  (iii) Gripping with hands and arms
  (iv) Pushing and lifting with hands and arms i.e. under partner.
Partners explore all possible grips and select appropriately for the task that is set (see p. 150).

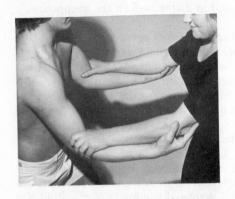

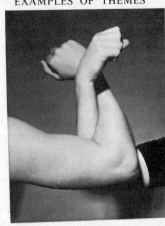

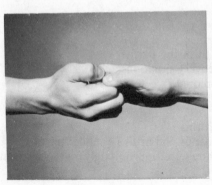

B. Intermediate apparatus

Mats and forms.
 (i) Practise spinning jumps off forms on to mats, recover with roll (turn both ways). Use arms to turn body.
 (ii) Use arms to gain height in jumping, and land.
 (iii) Balance on forms; with weight on bent arms recover on mat.
 (iv) Balance on forms; with weight on straight arms, turn or twist and recover on mat.
 (v) Explore all ways of taking weight on hands on form, and on form and floor, selecting appropriate recovery.
 (vi) Help partner maintain balance on form while taking weight:
   a) on hands
   b) on other parts

C. Large apparatus (fig. 20)

1. Ropes, Rope ladder, trapeze etc.
   Task. a) Practise swinging and inversion on one rope, two ropes, ladder, trapeze.
   b) Hold one rope with left hand, run and jump, as jumping swing right arm up to grip rope above left, this will half turn body to left, drop off rope at height of swing.

2. Trampette. Bar 1 at stretch jump height, bar 1a at chest height. Mattress as shown.
   Task a) Take off trampette to catch high bar with
     (i) arms straight
     (ii) arms bent
     and hold still position before recovering on mattress.
   b) Practise forward and backward somersaults on low bar with
     (i) arms bent
     (ii) arms straight.

3. Two boxes, trampette, mats as shown.
   Task. Using any approach to either box, land on box with weight on hands

4. Two bars, 1 at knee height, 2 at shoulder height. One bench inclined onto each bar with mats as shown.
   Task. a) Low bench. Run up bench, swing through bars or over bars taking weight on hands on top bar. Recover on mat.
   b) High bench. Pull up bench, weight on hands on lower bar to · recover.

5. Horse. Two mats as shown.

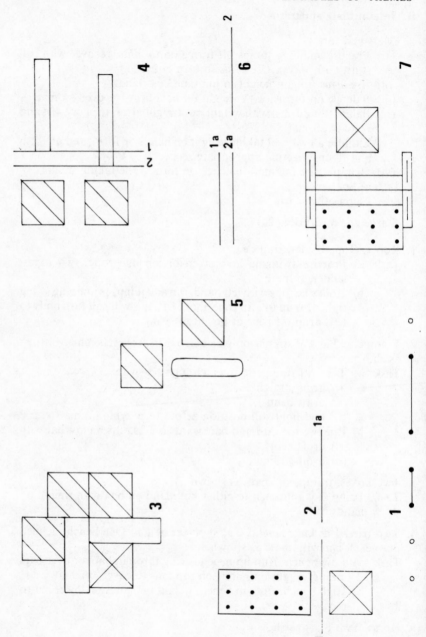

Task. In twos or threes. Help partner recover from any vault involving weight on hands on the horse.

6. Three bars, 2 at jump stretch height, 1a at head height, 2a at hip height.
   Task. a) Travel along high bar on hands with body swing either side to side or forwards and backwards.
   b) Find ways of turning between the bars 1a and 2a with one hand gripping the top bar, one the bottom bar.
   c) Swing over the top bar, coming down to the ground through the two bars 1a and 2a.

7. Trampette, trestles at two heights, mattress.
   Task. Take weight on stepped surface using hands or arms to support or grip.

13 SWINGING

THEME: **Swinging**   CLASSIFICATION: **Action**
                                  GROUP: **Advanced**

SELECTION

Although aspects of this theme can be included when working on transference of weight, use of the theme on its own should follow the achievement of skill in flight and landing. The class should also possess a degree of arm strength and confidence in inversion.

DEFINITION

Swinging involves moving around, or to and fro about a fixed point. The theme emphasises two distinct ways: by gripping or weight-bearing to form a fixed point, it can swing non-weight-bearing parts of the body to initiate another movement; or, the whole body can swing with a piece of apparatus which has a fixed point, such as a rope. Swinging makes use of gravity and the weight of the free body parts and their distribution about the fixed point.

AIMS

1. To encourage the use of swinging momentum of parts of the body in initiating travelling movements and flight.
2. To develop skill and safety on swinging apparatus, using moments of stillness at the end of the swing, for eventual use in complex apparatus situations. This theme tends to be concentrated on apparatus work and can often be used to develop confidence on large apparatus.
3. To develop awareness of the effects of the distribution of the body parts about the fixed point of the swing.

OBJECTIVES

1. **An individual floor** sequence to include use of swinging arms and legs to initiate travelling, flying and turning movements.
2. **Mats and forms.** A sequence to include:
   (i) Use of swinging leg to initiate flight onto, off and over form and to achieve balance
   (ii) Use of swinging arms to initiate flying, travelling and turning movements and to achieve balance.
3. **Partner sequence** to include:
   (i) Matching individual swinging movements
   (ii) Following partner in individual swinging movements
   (iii) Contrasting individual swinging movements
   (iv) Assisting a partner into flight, turns or balance using swinging movement
   (v) Swinging a partner round or to and fro and continuing into individual movements.
4. Set tasks on swinging apparatus—ropes, rings, trapeze, ladders, to use moment of stillness at end of swing to land safely on mats.
5. As 4 above, to land on forms and other flat surfaces, and using moment of stillness to move from static apparatus to swinging apparatus.
6. Chosen sequence on large apparatus.

MOVEMENT MATERIAL I   EXPLORATION OF THEME

A. Using arms
   (i) Swinging arms upwards to take the body into a high jump.
   (ii) Swinging arms forwards to take the body into a broad jump.
   (iii) Swinging arms to one side of the body to recoil into a turning jump.
   (iv) Swinging arms to one side of the body to recoil into a spin (e.g. on heel or seat).
   (v) Swinging arms across the body to go into sideways jump or turn.

B. Using legs
   (i) Place hands on floor in front: swing one leg up behind to take the weight on the hands.
   (ii) Use of swinging leg to take weight on hands in cartwheels and other agilities.
   (iii) Swing one leg up behind to take hands and trunk down into controlled fall.
   (iv) Use of swinging leg to take body high, e.g. 'western roll' and 'straddle' type jumps.

(v) Use of swinging leg to take body into turns, twists and spins.

MOVEMENT MATERIAL II   DEVELOPMENT OF THEME

A. Partner work
  (i) Partners copy each others' swinging movements, attempting to match movement.
  (ii) Patners work on contrasting swinging movements, e.g. A swings leg, B swings arm; A uses left side, B right side.
  (iii) A assisting B into flight or turns, using swinging movements.
  (iv) A swinging B round and to and fro, to continue into individual movements.

B. Intermediate apparatus
  (i) Mats and forms: use of swinging leg to initiate: flight on to, over and off form; turns; travelling along form.
    Use of swinging arms to initiate: flight on to, over and off form; turns, turning jumps; and travelling.
  (ii) Ropes and mats: (Fig. 21)
    a) Pull rope back and allow to swing straight: watch for moment of stillness at end of swing.
    b) Run with rope and swing up with it: turn and land on the mats at the end of the swing by swinging up and twisting around legs or one leg. Gradually move the mats further away from the ropes so that there needs to be a longer swing, and landing from a greater height. Vary body shape to assess effect on swing.
    c) On still ropes, use of leg swing to go upside-down: assess affect of body shape.

C. Large apparatus
  1. Ropes opposite form and box with mats between.
  2. Ropes opposite single bars, one high, one low, with upturned benches between.
  3. Horse with no pommels, 2 benches, 1 upturned bench, mats.
  4. Double bars, hip height and 'easy reach' height, with form parallel to bars and end on to box, mats.
  5. Trapeze and rope ladder opposite double bars, hip height and 'easy reach' height, box end on to bars, with two vertical poles at its other end, mats.

Tasks. These general tasks apply to all apparatus settings.
1. As B(ii) above, landing on forms and other flat surfaces at the end of the swing. This task should be attempted only when there is full control of

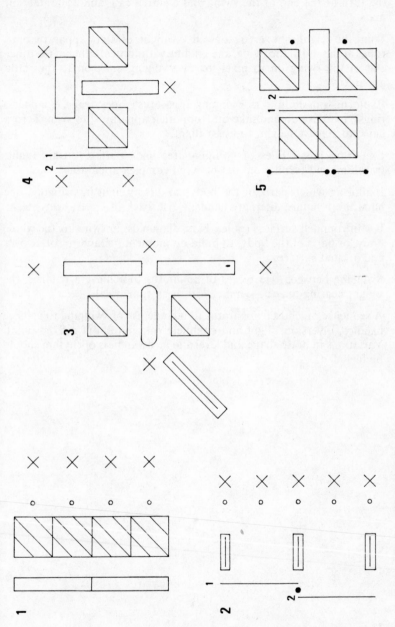

Fig. 21. Swinging—large apparatus layout.

the turn at the end of the swing and children can land accurately on mats.

2. Using the height of boxes, trestles, etc., swinging off static apparatus onto ropes at the end of the swing, and landing with control either at the other end of the swing on to mats, or by swinging back on to the static apparatus.

3. Exploring possibilities of swinging apparatus (ropes, trapeze, ladders, rings): to arrive on and take off from other apparatus; to swing across gaps; to achieve height, to assist flight.

4. Exploring possibilities of swinging free body parts to attain flight, travelling and turning on and between complex apparatus.

5. Exploring which parts of the body can take weight in swinging: one hand, both hands, alternate hands, waist, back of knees, heels etc.

6. Use of rounded surfaces (poles, bars, diagonals) in swinging the whole body, or parts of the body, to build up momentum, and to rotate over and around surfaces.

7. Swinging between two pieces of apparatus to achieve a balance: the weight bearing may be symmetrical or asymmetrical.

8. A sequence on chosen apparatus to include use of swinging to achieve balance, inversion, flight and complete rotation about a fixed point. Variations in body shape and level and an awareness of rhythm should be included.

14 SYMMETRY AND ASYMMETRY

THEME: **Symmetry/Asymmetry** CLASSIFICATION: **Body**
                                 GROUP: **Advanced**

SELECTION

This theme could be chosen for a class of children who are proficient in twisting and turning movements and confident in different types of balance. The theme might be used in order to encourage the accuracy of symmetrical movements, or the variety of asymmetrical movements. It could also be used to encourage the use of each side of the body separately.

DEFINITION

Symmetry of the body occurs when right and left sides of the body match exactly, either in a held position or during locomotion: symmetrical movement is confined to up, down, forward and backward, rocking and rolling movements and demands accuracy and discipline.

The body is asymmetrical in stillness or locomotion when one side of the body is stressed so that it does not match the other: the stress can be made on either side of the body, or it can be alternated, as in everyday actions like walking and running. In such movements there is symmetry through time, but not in action. The role of the subordinate side of the body is important for weight-bearing and balance purposes. Children can be asked to stress the 'non-favourite' side of their bodies in order to extend their range of movement and to counter the habitual use of one side of the body. It is important that a distinction is made between the weight-bearing and free parts of the body: a balance may have a symmetrical base with the rest of the body in symmetry or asymmetry; but it is not possible for the rest of the body to be symmetrical over an asymmetrical base.

AIMS

1. To encourage an awareness of symmetry and asymmetry in stillness and locomotion.
2. To experience balance, transference of weight, flight, rocking and rolling in symmetry.
3. To develop confidence in balance on asymmetrical bases.
4. To experience stress of either side of the body, and, if necessary, to encourage use of the neglected side of the body.
5. To promote an awareness of the importance of the non-stressed side of the body.
6. To encourage accuracy and extend variety of movement.
7. To use alternate sides of the body in controlled locomotion.
8. To encourage an awareness of the pathways associated with symmetrical and asymmetrical use of the body.

OBJECTIVES

1. **Individual floor sequence** to include symmetrical balances and movements, stresses of each side of the body in balance and locomotion and alternate stresses.
2. **Mats and benches**: a sequence, utilising at the same time the surfaces of form and mat to show asymmetrical bases for balance and locomotion, in contrast to symmetrical balances and travelling along or over the form or mat.
3. **Partner sequence**, to show matching symmetrical movements and individual asymmetrical movements to show composite symmetrical shapes.
4. **Intermediate apparatus** a) to develop skill in utilising the surfaces of single pieces of apparatus (e.g. low box, horse etc.) to use asymmetrical and symmetrical bases for balance and to explore the effect of different body shapes above those bases. b) to develop skill in stressing alternate sides of the body travelling, e.g. on ropes, ladders, bars, window ladders.

5.)
6.) Any two sequences chosen from large apparatus.

MOVEMENT MATERIAL I   EXPLORATION OF THEME

A. Symmetry
  (i) In stillness:
    a) Explore the different positions possible while matching the sides of the body e.g. 'star', 'pin', 'tuck', 'straddle'.

b) Using symmetrical bases, explore the symmetrical ways in which the body can balance over the base, e.g. 2 hands, 2 feet, head and hands, knees.

(ii) In movement:

a) Jump from two feet to two feet: explore asymmetrical/symmetrical body shapes in the air and their effects on flight and landing.

b) Explore ways of transferring weight from feet to hands and back to feet, moving symmetrically.

c) Explore ways of symmetrical rocking and rolling to initiate or recover from another movement, which may stress one side in contrast, e.g. backward roll into balance on one knee; landing from turning jump into forward roll.

d) Using methods already explored, travel along a straight pathway, matching the movements of both sides of the body.

B. Asymmetry

(i) In stillness:

a) Using symmetrical bases, explore the effect of different asymmetrical body shapes on the way in which balance is maintained.

b) Use different body parts to form an asymmetrical base for balances.

c) Consider what the unstressed side of the body is doing to maintain balance.

d) Gradually decrease the size of the asymmetrical base (e.g. to one hand, one foot) and consider the body position needed to hold the balance.

(ii) In movement:

a) Stressing each side of the body, explore taking weight on non-matching parts of the body.

b) Transfer weight between non-matching parts of the body: vary the side of the body stressed, e.g. left knee to right shoulder; right shoulder to left hip.

c) Jump from one foot to two feet, two feet to one foot, left foot to right foot, right foot to left foot.
Try to develop timing and spring from your 'non-favourite' foot.

d) Jump, showing symmetrical body shapes in the air: how do they affect flight and landing?

e) Use stress on one side of the body to initiate a twist or turn, e.g. by recoil of arms.

f) Reduce an asymmetrical base to take the body out of balance,

e.g. balancing on knee and hand, remove the hand.
g) Use rolling and rocking movements, changing the side of the body stressed to imitate a change of direction.
h) Stressing different sides of the body, travel along an indirect pathway.

C. Alternate Movement

Stress alternate sides of the body in repetitive actions like crawling, running and walking. Discover other actions which can be used in this way to travel, e.g. climbing, gripping and releasing.

D. Complementary use of Symmetrical and Asymmetrical Movement

a) Some symmetrical balances need asymmetrical use of the body to achieve them (e.g. handstands). Try both asymmetrical and symmetrical ways of moving into the balance and out of it.
b) Use alternate sides of the body to travel into an asymmetrical balance, then into a symmetrical balance.
c) In some sideways movements (e.g. cartwheel) asymmetrical movement results in a symmetrical body position over the point of support. Explore actions, where this happens e.g. sideways 'bunny hop', sideways roll over the shoulders.

MOVEMENT MATERIAL II   DEVELOPMENT OF THEME

A. Partner work

(i) Facing partner, mirror symmetrical movements while travelling to meet.
(ii) Following partner, match asymmetrical movements.
(iii) Make individual asymmetrical shapes which make a symmetrical shape when joined with a partner.

B. Intermediate Apparatus

(i) Mats and benches (see tasks on p. 119-20)
(ii) Single low pieces of apparatus with mats: box, horse, buck etc.
   a) Explore ways of balancing on symmetrical bases, using one or more surfaces.
   b) Explore ways of balancing on asymmetrical bases, using more than one level on the apparatus (e.g. weight on hands, one gripping pommel and one gripping leg of horse) and coming off balance safely.
   c) Explore ways of arriving on and getting off apparatus symmetrically.

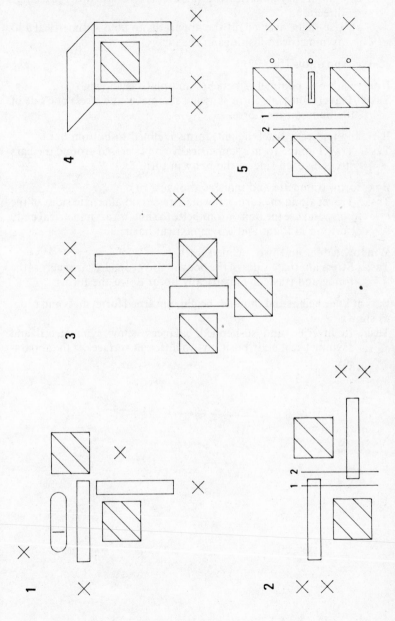

Fig. 22. Symmetry and asymmetry—large apparatus layout.

   d) Explore asymmetrical arrivals and take-offs in order to change
      direction.
   e) Use flight over or off the apparatus to hold symmetrical and
      asymmetrical positions in the air.

C. Large Apparatus (fig. 22)

1. Horse with one pommel, 2 benches and mats as shown.
   Task. Travel along one form showing symmetry and stress one side of
   the body on the horse.

2. Bars, hip and easy reach height, forms inclined to bottom bar.
   Task. Travel up the form symmetrically and over and around the bars
   stressing each side of the body in turn.

3. Box, form, trampette and mats as shown.
   Task. Travel along the form showing stresses on alternate sides of the
   body and use the box or trampette to show an asymmetrical body
   position in flight and a symmetrical balance.

4. Window ladder and two inclined forms.
   Task. Stress alternate sides of the body to travel up, down, or across the
   frame and travel symmetrically up or down the forms.

5. Bars at knee height and shoulder height, upturned form, mats and ropes
   as shown.
   Task. In inverted and suspended balances, show symmetrical and
   asymmetrical body positions on different surfaces of the apparatus.

15 THREES AND SMALL GROUPS

THEME: **Threes and Small Groups** CLASSIFICATION **Relationship**
                                       GROUP: **Advanced**

SELECTION

This theme is for secondary children or students who are mature enough to take responsibility and also to submit to leadership. It is useful for students who are intelligent and inventive but who are not very able performers, who can gain more satisfaction from working with others than in individual performance. The group situation offers interesting problems in combining work which needs highly skilled performance with simpler actions of the less able. Some of the work is only suitable for men.

DEFINITION

This theme is an extension of work in twos. It develops the idea of two (or more) people controlling the balance, flight and falling, the lifting, carrying and placing of the third person. It extends the spatial and rhythmic patterning possibilities and the use of partners as mobile and ejective apparatus.

AIMS

1. Cooperation in group situations.
2. Extension of movement vocabulary and experience.

OBJECTIVES

1. **Floor sequence.** In a group of five.
   The aim of this sequence is to make a pattern of movements which will

look effective and pleasing from the viewpoint of an onlooker. The sequence will therefore be addressed to a specific direction and the group will be concerned with:

(i) Group shape

(ii) Choice of simple body shapes, which will look pleasing when repeated by other bodies in a close group formation. The movement should be a matching one.

The requirements are:

    a) Matching body shape

    b) Matching group rhythm

    c) Matching group direction and level

2. **Mats and forms.**

In threes. Two sequences. Groups arrange own apparatus.

(i) One member of the group leads the movement pattern. This is followed exactly by the other members of the group in a file (i.e. follow my leader). Each member of the group leads in turn. The pattern of movement must be continuous, therefore movements causing the change in leadership are important.

(ii) A sequence illustrating several ways of two people lifting a third including:

    a) helping him to jump

    b) turning him

    c) throwing him

3.
4. } **Large apparatus** (diagram p. 169)
5.

All work in groups of five or more. Each group must take part in three sequences:

(i) one involving lifting and throwing a person

(ii) one involving carrying and throwing a person

(iii) one where apparatus is shared - all members of the group working at once.

MOVEMENT MATERIAL I   EXPLORATION OF THEME

A. **Working in threes**

  (i) **With no body contact**

    a) Using body actions, all three working in unison

    b) Using body actions, all three working in canon

    c) Emphasising change of speed, two follow the leader

  (ii) **With body contact.** Two forming apparatus for lifting (Fig. 19-1)

1

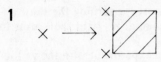

Fig. 23.1

Two people making supports for the third to jump between. The person jumping uses the shoulders of the supports to 'push off' to gain extra height.

2

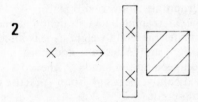

Fig. 23.2

The supports may stand astride the form or on it. They turn to face the third person who runs and jumps over the form. The supports, using a shakehand grip (see pp. 150) and gripping the elbow, lift the mover high over the form.

3

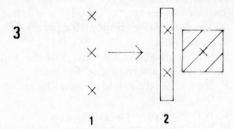

Fig. 23.3

1   **2**

Using the same grip as in 2, the supports run with the mover, lifting him and throwing him over the gap and continue with him.

4

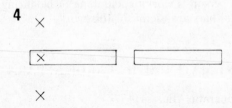

Fig. 23.4

Here the supports run with the mover, lift him over the gap, continue with him to assist the slowing down and recovery.

    (iii) **Two form support for turning the third**
- a) Two can make a bar with their arms for the third to use as apparatus.
- b) The two can experiment with the various grips (see p. 150) to help the third to turn or spin.

B. Working in small groups.
  (i) **Lifting and carrying**
- a) As a group lift 'body' and replace:
  the group - keeping backs straight and bending knees, should move under the body weight as it is lifted.
  the body - should be taut and must maintain a horizontal position keeping the hands by the sides.
- b) Lift body above heads of group - practise gently throwing and catching body.
- c) Try a) and b) with body forming other body shapes.
- d) Try a) and b) with body in upright position.
- e) Carry body and put it down somewhere else.

  (ii) **Throwing and catching a body**
- a) Throwing the body. Two or more lift a body to catch a high bar, or moving rope, or onto other apparatus.
- b) Two or more support a body as it falls from a platform. In making themselves responsible for the falling weight the group must consider:
  1. Which are the nearest parts of the body.
  2. How and where to grip the body.
  3. How to turn the body so that he arrives back gently on his feet.
  4. Is there a pivoting point?
  5. Which parts of the body may be gripped safely to break speed.

  (iii) **Lifting and moving apparatus**
The group finds ways of lifting and turning apparatus on which one person is working, climbing or balancing. Forms, poles and metal bars are useful for this work.

MOVEMENT MATERIAL II   LARGE APPARATUS

A. Large apparatus (fig. 24)

1. Two boxes, horse, trampette, mats (any number) as shown.
Task. The group keeps up a continuous movement on and off boxes

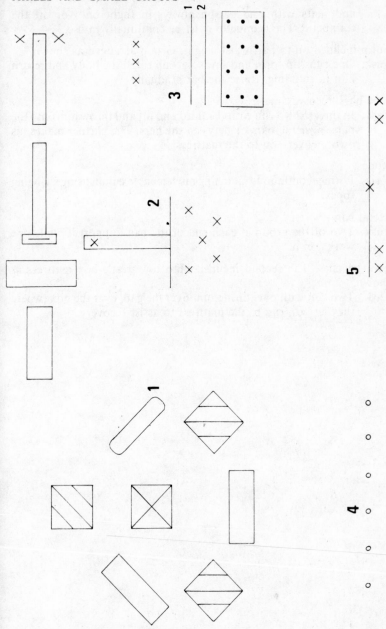

Fig. 24. Groups—large apparatus layout.

and mats with one person always in flight onto or off the trampette. The trampette must be continually in use.

2. Form inclined on to bar, waist height. Group arranged as shown.
   Task. One runs up form and dives - group catch the body and return him to standing. Raise the bar gradually.

3. Two bars, recovery mattress.
   Task. In threes. Two run with the third and lift and throw him onto the bars, over the bars or between the bars. The partner makes his own recovery on to the mattress.

4. Ropes.
   Task. Form a continuous matching movement in canon using swinging ropes.

5. Metal bar.
   Task. Two of the group at each end of the bar, support it while one works on it.

6. Two benches. The second inclined onto low trestle-box mattress as shown.
   Task. Two run with one, lifting him over the gap, over the box (where they let go), run to the mattress to assist recovery.

16 RHYTHMIC PATTERNS

THEME: **Rhythmic Patterns** CLASSIFICATION: **Dynamics**
  GROUP **Advanced**

SELECTION

This theme might be chosen for a specific purpose, such as a demonstration of work. It should be taken with highly skilled people who are accustomed to working in partners or groups. It will give an added dimension to the composition of movement sequences as it takes the various factors of rhythmic phrasing into account. Some of the simpler ideas should of course be included in early themes.

DEFINITION

This theme involves the study of accent, timing, repetition and phrasing and its use in the composition of movement sequences. The emphasis of the theme is away from the action and function of the body and on to the rhythms and sounds made by the body or several bodies in movement.

AIMS

The aims of the theme are:
1. To encourage a sense of timing and phrasing in the composition of movement sequences,
2. To give experience in conforming to a variety of set rhythmic patterns,
3. To experience the effect of change of accent on a certain movement phrase,
4. To develop the aesthetic sense of phrasing, rise and fall of accent and rhythm in individual and group sequences of movement.

OBJECTIVES

1. **Floor sequence.**
   A common class rhythm must be maintained through the sequence. This will be repeated three or four times and contain:
   a) a common class movement, conforming to the rhythm
   b) a variety of individual sequences, conforming to the rhythm
   c) a partner or group sequence, conforming to the rhythm
2. **Partner sequence.**
   Each pair selects a rhythmic phrase and builds up a sequence in the following order:
   a) matching movement conforming to timing of phrase
   b) A moves to phrase, B keeps still
   c) B moves to phrase, A keeps still
   d) both move to phrase
   e) A moves to first half of phrase, B to second half
   f) B moves to first half of phrase, A to second half
   g) repeat (d)
   h) repeat (a)

   NB. The phrase will be repeated eight times altogether.
3. **Intermediate apparatus sequences.**
   Mats and forms to be arranged by the students.
   a) A sequence of movement in threes, using a rhythm in canon. (See p. 175)
   b) A group rhythm to be maintained while everybody is working at once sharing the apparatus.
4. **Large apparatus.**
   a) Five sharing apparatus, conforming to the same rhythm but not to the same movement sequence.
5. Three sequences to show acceleration, deceleration and climax with:
   a) the climax in the middle of the sequence
   b) the climax at the beginning of the sequence
   c) the climax at the end of the sequence
6. Teacher dictates class rhythm. All students working using all apparatus.

MOVEMENT MATERIAL I: EXPLORATION OF THEME

KEY TO SYMBOLS:

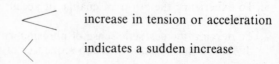

increase in tension or acceleration

indicates a sudden increase

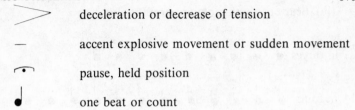

deceleration or decrease of tension

accent explosive movement or sudden movement

pause, held position

one beat or count

A. Teacher sets and maintains rhythm while class:

(i)   using travelling actions (see p. 79), start from standing, build movement up to a climax, hold a still position and repeat.

(ii) using travelling actions build up speed, change action on the accent and follow this by a slowing down movement and repeat.

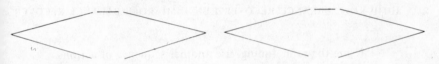

B. Individual sets own rhythm and varies the timing:

(i)   A quick action leading to a climax, long slowing down process.

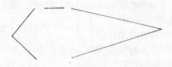

(ii) A slow build-up to a climax, followed by a quick recovery to stillness.

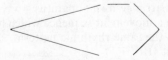

(iii) Beat out rhythmic phrase on the floor:

a) in threes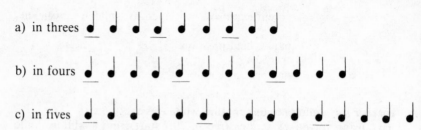

b) in fours

c) in fives

> and then make a stepping or jumping pattern to it. Try other
> actions to the rhythms.

(iv) Make an action sequence. Determine the phrasing and accent
according to the sequence; e.g. Run, jump with turn, roll into
balance, recover slowly and repeat.

RUN JUMP ROLL BALANCE RECOVER RUN JUMP ROLL BALANCE RECOVER

Using the same timing, use another sequence of actions.

MOVEMENT MATERIAL II   DEVELOPMENT OF THEME

A. Partner work.

(i) Teacher sets a repetitive rhythm which has two parts.
A's move on first part   ⎫
B's move on second part ⎬ · and reverse the process

(ii) Pairs select own rhythm and use it for:
matching movements
one partner moving at a time
each partner moving in a different part of the phrase
different movement sequences to same rhythm

B. Intermediate apparatus.

Students select and arrange own apparatus:
In threes. Compose a movement sequence which has three parts, each
part conforming to the same rhythmic pattern.
Part I, Part II, Part III.

The sequences should be performed in canon thus:

A	Part I	Part II	Part III	I	II
B		Part I	Part II	III	I
C			I	II	III

and continue.

C. Large apparatus
(i) In fives

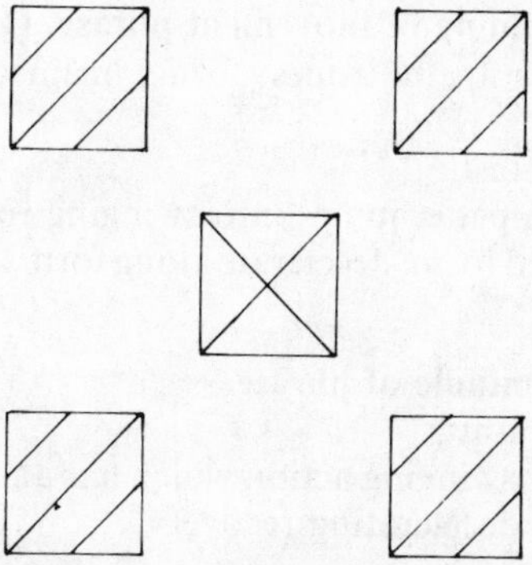

Fig. 25.

Group of five (or one more than the number of mats). Keep one person in flight to or from trampette. All moving between mat and mat or mat and trampette.

(ii) In twos
Swing backwards and forwards on a rope.

A develops rhythm—
Run
Take off
Turn in air
Run in opposite direction
Take off
Turn in air
Repeat.

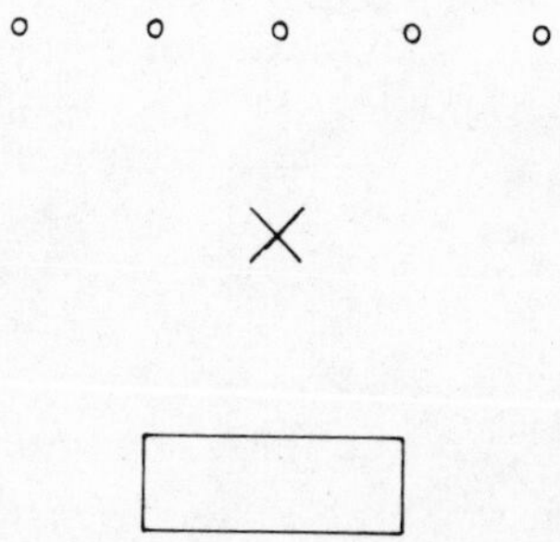

B keeping in same rhythm (Fig. 26);
Run
Take off
Land on box
Turn
Repeat in opposite direction

A and B keeping in time.

Fig. 26.

(iii) **In a group**
Choose own apparatus. A leads group in a series of actions over the apparatus, the rest of the group follow-my-leader. Each person takes it in turn to lead. Determine method of changing leadership and keep action going.

(iv) **Individual**
Accent on beginning of movement phrase. (Fig. 27)
High trestle, trampette, ropes, forms inclined down and away from ropes, mats.
Begin on high trestle
Drop onto trampette, jump onto swinging rope,
Land on inclined form, decelerate along form to mat and slowly resolve to standing.

(v) **Accent in middle of phrase.**
Select own apparatus.
Any vaulting or swinging action which has an acceleration followed by a climax and a decelerating recovery.

(vi) **Accent at end of phrase**
Select own apparatus.
Any action that builds up to top speed and maximum tension and ends with a sudden stop in a held position.

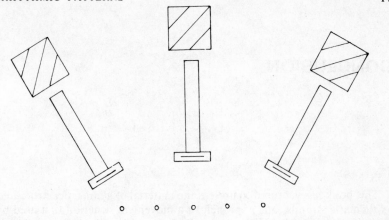

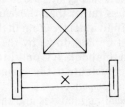

Fig. 27. Apparatus layout.

CONCLUSION

This book has ventured to present the material of gymnastics structured as thematic strands, one approach to a movement situation first used by Rudolf Laban (1879–1958) in his book Modern Educational Dance (1948).

The thematic approach to gymnastics is particularly suitable where the teacher is in contact with a group of pupils of mixed physical ability; furthermore, it is appropriate in a gymnastic situation where the aim is the extension of body awareness rather than the learning of externally predetermined skill sequences. Individual freedom in the choice of movement by the pupil within the structure laid down by the teacher is the essence of gymnastics as presented in this book. It is only in this way that each student is able to learn from and contribute to the gymnastics lesson whatever his physical endowment and experience.

It is hoped that the preceding analyses and theme suggestions will give constructive support to the teacher whose concern is with the achievement by his students of the aims of educational gymnastics. The author believes the achievement of these aims to be essential to the full and mature development of the normal human being.

REFERENCES

BARTLETT, F.C. *Remembering* Cambridge, England: Cambridge University Press, 1932

BEARDSLEY, M.C. *The possibility of criticism* Wayne U.P. 1970.

BENNETT, D.H. The body concept. *J. Ment. Sci.* 1960, **106,** 56–75.

HEAD, SIR H. *Studies in Neurology* London, Hodder & Stoughton Ltd. 1920, Vol. II, 605–609.

HUXLEY, A. *Ends and Means* London: Chatto & Windus 1938.

LABAN, R. *Modern Educational Dance* London, Macdonald and Evans, 1948.

MEREDITH, G.D. *Instruments of Communication* Oxford: Pergamon 1966.

MORGAN, R. *Concerns & Values in Physical Education* London G. Bell & Sons 1974.

NASH, J. *Developmental Psychology* N.J.: Prentice-Hall 1970.

PIAGET, J. & INHELDER *The growth of logical thinking* London: Routledge & Kegan Paul, 1958.

RICOEUR, P. *Freedom &·Nature* North Western U.P. 1966.

RYLE, G. *The Concept of Mind,* Penguin Harmondsworth: 1949.

SCHMIDT, R.A. A schema theory of discrete motor skill learning in *Psychological Review* 1975 8 **4**.

TYLDESLEY, D. Unpublished paper on motor control in skilled performance. Leeds University, 1975.

VYGOTSKY, L.S. *Thought and Language*, Cambridge, Mass: MIT Press, 1962.

WRIGHT, J. Composition in gymnastics *Focus on Gymnastics* APWCPE Conference Papers 1975–6.

INDEX

Action 29
Aesthetics 1, 7, 13–5, 24, 102, 147
Aims, of
  apparatus 75
  book 2f
  gymnastics 6f
  teacher 17, 75
  theme 26   see also individual
    themes
Apparatus 5, 36, 38, 48
  choosing 60–1
  coaching 71–2
  intermediate 35–7
  introduction 64
  large 39   see also individual themes
  lesson 67
  organisation 61–3
  to floor work 70–1
  use of 39, 59–75

Balance/Overbalance
  analysis (of theme) 43–52
Body action 29–30, 19–24
  awareness 7–8, 17
  concept 8–9
  schema 7
  shape 116–21
  with partners 20, 29–30, 32–5

Dynamics 20–4, 31–2

Exploration
  of theme 28–32, 44–5
  see also individual themes

Falling 92, 135–9
Feet and Legs 96–100
Flight 108–15

Grips 150
Groups 35, 165

Hands and Arms 147–53

Jumping 89–90

Lesson(s) 53–8
  plan 56–7
  apparatus 67–8

Levels and Directions 140–45
Locomotion and Pause 78–82

Master plan 47, 49–52
Movement
  concepts 10–3, 17
  material 28f   see also individual
    themes
  phrase 19
  schemata 10–1

Objectives
  of themes 18–9, 27–8, 40   see also
    individual themes
Observation 3, 65, 72
Olympic gymnastics 1
Organisation 55–8, 61, 67–8

Partner work 32–5, 122–37 see also
    individual themes
Pathways 142–3
Performance 14–5, 26, 41, 75

Relationships
  in body action 21–2
  in partner work 32–5, 122f
  in group work 165–70
Rising and Falling 135–9
Rocking 90–1
Rolling 91–2
Rhythmic Pattern 171–77

Safety
  in gymnasium 55, 61, 66
  on apparatus 25, 63–4, 166–8
Sequences 18–9, 40–2, 53   see also
    individual themes
Skills 1, 7, 9–10, 13
Speed, changes of 102–6
Symmetry and Asymmetry 119,
    159–64
Swinging 154–9

Tasks 18–9, 39–40   see also
    individual themes
Themes
  advanced 23
  analysis of 25–42
  apparatus for 69–70

Themes, contd.
    classification of 21–2
    concept of 16–24
    definition of 26, 42   see also
        individual themes
    development of 32f
    example of 42–52
    hierarchy of 22–4
    intermediate 23
    introductory 23
    model for 3

    selection of 25–6, 43   see also
        individual themes
Trampette, use of 113
Twisting and Turning 89–90, 128–34

Work units 2–3, 47, 55–7
Weight-bearing 84–7
    on hands 85
    on head 86
    transference 88–95